KU-079-895

Acknowledgements

I T IS A pleasure to be able to thank two friends and colleagues, Douglas Porch of the Naval Postgraduate School, who suggested I write this book; and Thomas Henrickson of the Hoover Institution at Stanford University, without whose support it could not have been done. I am also much obliged to Penny Gardiner for her good-humoured forbearance and professionalism in putting this volume together; and to Malcolm Swanston for his splendid cartography.

A more general sort of thanks is also in order to all those whose hard-won contributions to our knowledge of modern war must go unacknowledged in a book that, by its nature, cannot support the normal apparatus by which credit is given where it is due. I am painfully aware of how many fine scholars will find their achievements reflected in these pages. You know who you are. I only wish to say that I do too.

DANIEL MORAN
Monterey, California

WARS OF NATIONAL LIBERATION

WARS OF NATIONAL LIBERATION

DANIEL MORAN

General Editor: John Keegan

CASSELL

Cassell, Wellington House, 125 Strand, London WC2R 0BB
www.cassell.co.uk

First published in Great Britain, 2001
This paperback edition 2002

British Library Cataloguing-in-publication Data
ISBN: 0-304-36266-2

Cartography: Arcadia Editions Ltd
Designer: Richard Carr
Printed and bound in Spain

Title Page: *A South Vietnamese soldier aims at a burning building near the Bien Hoa
Bridge on the outskirts of Saigon.*

Overleaf: *US forces in Saigon after the Tet Offensive, 1968.*

Contents

KEY TO MAPS

Military units–size

XXXXX ☐	army group
XXXX ☐	army
XXX ☐	corps
XX ☐	division
X ☐	brigade
III ☐	regiment
II ☐	battalion
⊠	infantry

Geographical symbols

▰	urban area
——	road
▬▬	railway
——	river
- - -	seasonal river
⊔⊔⊔⊔	canal
━━	border
⋈	bridge or pass

Military movements

➤	attack
◆-➤	retreat
✈	air attack
※	clash/attack
⊕	airfield

Map list

Chronology 1945–75

1945

Algeria	Sétif uprising (May).
China	Russia declares war on Japan. Manchuria occupied by Soviet forces (August–September).
Indonesia	Republic of Indonesia proclaimed (August). War between Indonesian People's Army and Dutch and British forces (October). Surabaya falls to British forces (November).
Middle East	British Government renews limits on Jewish immigration to Palestine. Jewish terrorism escalates sharply (October).
Korea	Soviet (August) and US (September) forces occupy Korean peninsula above and below the 38th Parallel.
Malaya	British Military Administration established. Communists disarmed (September).
Vietnam	Japanese coup displaces French administration (March). Republic of Vietnam proclaimed by Ho Chi Minh (September).

1946

Middle East	Irgun terrorists destroy King David Hotel in Jerusalem (July).
Kenya	Kenya African Union founded.
Vietnam	French troops replace Chinese in the North (March). Republic of Cochin-China proclaimed in the South (June). Fountainebleau Conference (July). French warships shell Haiphong (November).

1947

China	Lin Piao's Manchuria offensive begins (January).
Asia	India and Pakistan granted independence from Great Britain (August) amid massive civil unrest. Laos and Cambodia join the French Union as autonomous members (December).
Indonesia	West Java declares independence (May). Dutch offensive (July–August).
Madagascar	Anti-French rebellion begins (March).
Middle East	UN partition plan adopted (November). Escalating violence between Arabs and Jews follows.

1948

India	Gandhi assassinated (January).
Indonesia	Ceasefire follows Dutch capture of Jogjakarta (December).
Kenya	Mau Mau secret society founded.
Korea	North Korean People's Republic founded (May). Republic of South Korea founded (August). Guerrilla war begins in South Korea (November). Soviet occupation forces withdrawn (December).
Malaya	Federation of Malaya established (February). Serious communist resistance begins (April). State of emergency declared (June). 'Ferret Force' teams begin counter-guerrilla sweeps in jungle areas (September).
Middle East	State of Israel proclaimed. Open war begins (May). First UN truce (June). Israeli 'Ten Day Offensive' (July). Second UN truce (July–October).

1949

China	Communist forces enter Beijing (January). Mao Tse-tung proclaims People's Republic of China (October).
Indonesia	UN Security Council orders Netherlands to transfer sovereignty to Indonesian republicans (January). Ceasefire agreement. Dutch forces withdraw from Djakarta and Jogjakarta (May). Netherlands concedes Indonesian sovereignty (November).
Korea	Periodic border clashes begin along 38th Parallel (May). US occupation forces withdrawn (June).
Malaya	Malayan Communist Party publishes plan for establishment of Peoples' Democratic Republic of Malaya (February).
Middle East	First Arab–Israeli War ends in ceasefire (January–July).
Asia	Laos (July), Cambodia (November) and Vietnam (December) become Associated States of the French Union.

1950

Indonesia	Republic of Indonesia established (August). Incipient civil war between communist insurgents and national government persists until 1965.
Korea	Guerrilla insurgency in South Korea effectively suppressed

(May). North Korea invades South Korea (June). Pusan Perimeter (August). Inchon Landing (September). UN forces cross 38th Parallel. Large-scale Chinese infiltration south of the Yalu River begins (October). Chinese forces cross 38th Parallel (December).

Malaya	Briggs Plan begins (June).
Vietnam	Ho Chi Minh orders general mobilization (February). French outposts along Chinese border overrun by Viet Minh (October). 'De Lattre Line' established in the Red River delta (December).

1951

Korea	China rejects second UN ceasefire proposal (January). Allied counter-offensive begins (February). US forces cross 38th Parallel (March). Douglas MacArthur relieved. Chinese Spring Offensive (April). Armistice negotiations begin (July), suspended (August), resumed (October).
Malaya	High Commissioner Sir Henry Gurney killed (October).
Vietnam	Viet Minh Red River offensive (January–June). Viet Minh Black River campaign begins (November).

1952

Bolivia	National Revolutionary Movement seizes power (April).
Kenya	Mau Mau rebellion begins (October).
Korea	Communists reject UN proposal for voluntary repatriation of POWs (May). US air strikes on Yalu River power stations (June). Massive air raids on Pyongyang (August). Truce talks suspended (October).
Malaya	General Sir Gerald Templer appointed High Commissioner for Malaya. Comprehensive pacification campaign begins (February).
Philippines	Hukbalahap insurgency effectively suppressed (April).
Vietnam	French evacuate Hua Binh (February). Operation Lorraine, against supply system in Viet Bac region, fails to engage major enemy forces (October).

1953

Cuba	Fidel Castro's first attempt to overthrow Batista government fails (July).
Korea	Chinese accept voluntary repatriation of prisoners (March). Armistice negotiations resume. Sick and wounded prisoners exchanged (April). US and UN present final terms (May). South Korean President Rhee orders non-repatriating prisoners released (June). Armistice concluded (July).
Vietnam	Airhead at Dien Bien Phu established (November).

1954

Algeria	Algerian revolution begins (November).
Vietnam	Geneva Conference to negotiate a settlement to the Indo-China War announced (February). Siege of Dien Bien Phu begins (March). Geneva Conference begins (April). Dien Bien Phu falls (May). Partition agreement concluded (July).

1955

Algeria	Philippeville massacre (August).
Indonesia	Bandung Conference of twenty-nine Asian and African nations (April).
Vietnam	US agrees to train South Vietnamese Army.

1956

Cuba	Castro begins guerrilla operations in Sierra Maestra (December).
Middle East	Israeli forces seize Sinai Peninsula during Suez Crisis (October–November).
North Africa	French protectorates in Morocco and Tunisia independent (March).
Algeria	National Liberation Front (FLN) bombing campaign opens Battle of Algiers (September). Ben Bella and other FLN leaders hijacked and imprisoned (October).
Kenya	Last major operations against Mau Mau concluded (October).

1957

Algeria	French Army assumes responsibility for security in Algiers (January). Morice Line completed (September). Battle of Algiers ends (October).
Malaya	Independence (September).
Israel	Israeli forces complete withdrawal from Sinai. UN peacekeeping force deployed (March).
Vietnam	Communist insurgency, backed by Hanoi, begins in South Vietnam (October).

1958

Algeria	Sakiet air raid (February). *Pieds noirs* uprising (April–May). De Gaulle forms new French government (June).

1959

Algeria	Challe offensive (February–November). De Gaulle offers 'self-determination' for Algeria. FLN government in exile proclaimed in Cairo (September). Fifth French Republic established (December).
Cuba	Castro's guerrilla movement overthrows Batista government (January).
Vietnam	Organized infiltration of the South via Ho Chi Minh Trail and the sea begins (July). Intense repression of Communists in the South begins (August).

1960

Algeria	'Barricades Week' (January). Initial talks with FLN at Melun fail (June). UN recognizes Algeria's right to self-determination (December).
Congo	Independence (June). Katanga secedes (July). Lumumba overthrown by military coup (September).
Cuba	Soviet–Cuban friendship treaty (May).
Kenya	Official state of emergency ends (January).
Malaya	Official state of emergency ends (July).
Venezuela	Insurrection in Caracas nearly topples government (October).
Vietnam	North Vietnam introduces conscription (April). Military coup

against Diem fails (December). National Liberation Front for
South Vietnam founded in Hanoi (December).

1961

Algeria	Secret Army Organization (OAS) assassination campaign begins (January). Generals' coup in Algiers (April). Evian talks with FLN begin (May), fail (July).
Angola	War of independence begins.
Congo	Patrice Lumumba murdered (January). New national government established (August).
Cuba	Bay of Pigs invasion fails (April).
Kenya	Jomo Kenyatta released from detention.

1962

Algeria	Evian talks resume. Ceasefire agreement reached (March). OAS and FLN truce (June). Independence (July).
Cuba	Cuban missile crisis (October).
Venezuela	Rural insurgency begins (January).
Vietnam	Strategic hamlet programme.

1963

Congo	UN forces regain control in Katanga province (January).
Kenya	Independence (December).
Uruguay	Tupamaros founded.
Venezuela	Armed Forces of National Liberation (FALN) established (January).
Vietnam	Battle of Ap Bac (January). Diem assassinated (November).

1964

Africa	Organization of African Unity founded at Cairo (July).
Congo	Last UN forces withdrawn (June). Popular Army of Liberation forces take Stanleyville (August). US–Belgian intervention to rescue European hostages (November).
Middle East	Palestine Liberation Organization founded.
Venezuela	Amnesty offered to guerrilla insurgents and communists (March).
Vietnam	Tonkin Gulf resolution (August).

1965

Congo	Joseph Mobutu seizes power in *coup d'état* (November).
Asia	Border war between India and Pakistan (April–September).
Vietnam	US air attacks on North Vietnam ('Rolling Thunder') begin (February). First US combat troops deployed in Vietnam (March). Battle of Ia Drang Valley (October). US bombing campaign suspended (December).

1966

Middle East	Egyptian–Syrian defence pact (November).
Vietnam	US bombing campaign resumed (January). 'Search and destroy' operations begin (January).

1967

Bolivia	Che Guevara killed by Bolivian troops (October).
Middle East	Israeli–Syrian border clashes (April). UN forces withdrawn from Sinai at Egypt's request (May). Six Day War (June).
Vietnam	Operation Junction City (February–May). Operations around Khe Sanh begin (May). First major US anti-war demonstrations (September).

1968

Middle East	'War of Attrition' begins.
Vietnam	Seige of Khe Sanh (January–April). Tet Offensive (January–February). President Johnson announces he will not seek re-election. Bombing campaign suspended (March). Communist spring offensive. Peace talks begin in Paris (May).

1969

Middle East	Shelling and raids along Israeli–Egyptian frontier (March–July).
Vietnam	Major Communist offensive operations (February–March). 'Vietnamization' begins (March)

.

1970

Middle East	Final phase of 'War of Attrition' between Egypt and Israel (January–August) ends in ceasefire.
Vietnam	Secret talks between Henry Kissinger and Le Duc Tho begin (February). Major US operations in Cambodia (April–June).

1971

Asia	Post-election crisis in East Pakistan (March) leads to war between India and Pakistan (December).
Vietnam	US ground combat operations end (August). US air attacks against military targets in the North resume (December).

1972

Vietnam	US President Richard Nixon visits China (February). North Vietnamese 'Easter Offensive' (March). 'Linebacker I' air interdiction campaign (May–October). 'Christmas Bombing' of Hanoi (December).

1973

Middle East	Yom Kippur War (October).
Uruguay	Tupamaros defeated by Uruguayan military government.
Vietnam	Ceasefire declared (January). Last US troops leave Vietnam (March). Air operations against Cambodia ended by Congressional action (August).

1974

Vietnam	South Vietnamese President Thieu declares that 'war has resumed' (January). US President Richard Nixon resigns (August).

1975

Angola	Independence. Civil war begins (November).
Cambodia	Phnom Penh falls to Khmer Rouge (April).
Vietnam	Final North Vietnamese offensive begins (January). South Vietnam surrenders (April).

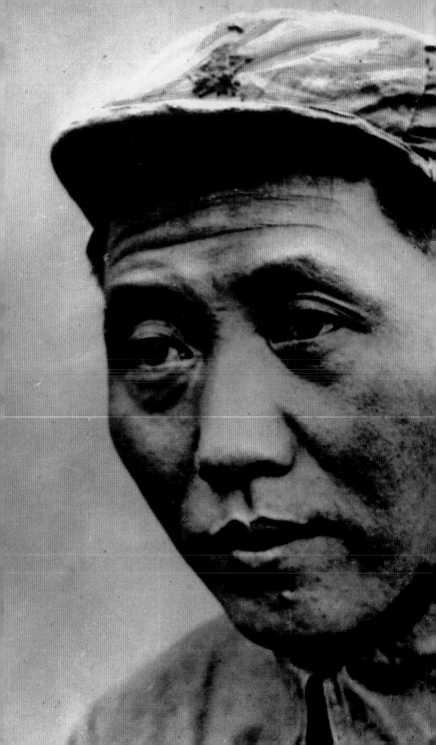

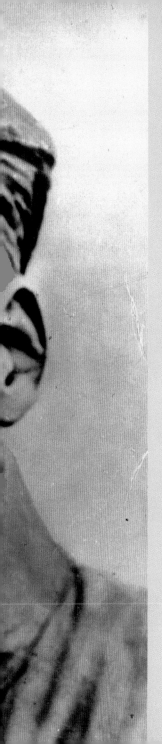

Nations
in Arms

*Mao Tse-tung, around the time of the Long March
(1934–5). 'A revolution,' he said, 'is not like inviting
people to dinner … To right a wrong, it is necessary
to exceed the proper limits.'*

Nations in Arms

> Modern bourgeois society, a society that has conjured up such gigantic means of production and exchange, is like the sorcerer who is no longer able to control the powers of the underworld that he has called up by his spells.
>
> *Karl Marx and Friedrich Engels,* The Communist Manifesto

THE WARS WITH which this book is concerned have usually been surveyed in volumes whose dust jackets feature the phrase 'since 1945'. It is a formula that captures the agnosticism that overcomes historians when they contemplate events so close at hand that the lens of historical study can barely resolve them. Yet there has never been any doubt that 'War since 1945' was a category that would have to disappear some day, and it is to the credit of the series editor that he has chosen to dispense with it. Which is not to deny that 1945 is a pivotal year. On the contrary: if anything, the passage of time has begun to clarify the nature of the inflection point marked by the end of the world wars, and also the limits of their influence. Whether 'Wars of National Liberation' will prove to be the best general characterization of the 'post-war wars' is impossible to say. It at least has the merit of taking seriously the professed aims of those who seized the initiative when Europe's global pre-eminence receded.

It has the defect of having been employed mainly as a euphemism. Like 'People's Republic', 'National Liberation' is a revolutionary slogan, designed to conceal sordid truths. It served to hurl back into the face of the oppressor the idea of the nation, which Europe invented, and the ideal of liberty, which the West cherishes above all others in politics, while deflecting attention from the methods and interests of the liberators themselves. Those thus assailed formulated brave, self-concealing euphemisms of their own, of which the most curious must be 'low intensity conflict', an expression that no one seriously acquainted with the fighting described here could possibly use without a grimace. The incongruities embedded in such phrases have not lessened with historical distance. Free societies have proved to be among the least common outcome of wars of national liberation; while such conflicts remain among the most worrisome in the eyes of professional soldiers called upon to fight them.

For present purposes, the framework of 'national liberation' is intended to be morally neutral, neither glamorous nor ironic, and as descriptively specific as the requirements of comprehensiveness allow. Most of the conflicts discussed represent unfinished business left over from the world wars. Some – those in China, Korea, Southeast Asia, and Palestine – were decisively shaped by the way the global conflict of 1914–45 played itself out in those places, and by the efforts of the victors to assert themselves afterwards. Others – in Africa and on the

The Big Four at the Versailles Peace Conference, 1919. From left to right, David Lloyd George of Great Britain, Naron Sonnino of Italy, Georges Clemenceau of France and Woodrow Wilson of the United States. Versailles' rhetorical embrace of 'national self-determination' as a sovereign principle of international relations proved to be a false dawn for the colonized world.

Mohandas Gandhi in 1930. Gandhi's campaign of non-violent civil disobedience became the moral centre of India's independence movement, and resonated strongly throughout the West. The strength of his example would prove insufficient to forestall the intense sectarian violence following the partition of Britain's Indian Empire in 1947.

Indian subcontinent – arose from the loosening of the European grip that the world wars helped bring about. Still others, in Latin America, deserve to be considered under the same rubric by virtue of the ideological and military affinities they display with contemporary warfare elsewhere; a point of view reinforced by the tendency of outsiders to view all these episodes as being of a piece. This perception had concrete consequences. Not the least significant element binding these conflicts together is their shared entanglement in the tendrils of the Cold War, in which they often played the role of proxy.

In most cases communist ideology provided a crucial stiffening to the sinews of national identity. This stiffening took two forms. On the one hand, communism made it easier for people to view their sacrifices not as transient acts of rebellion, like those known at all times, but as contributions to a historical process whose outcome was certain in the end. It is not easy to estimate the moral weight of such ideas, any more than it is easy to weigh the importance of Judgement Day in the history of Christianity. But to imagine that the millenarian qualities of Marxian communism played no part in sustaining national uprisings in our period is to set one's face against overwhelming evidence. The presumptive contradiction between cultural nation and social class that is so prominent in the history of European Marxism did not necessarily matter elsewhere, where communism often appeared to be just another tool of nation-building, capable of dissolving traditional structures while retaining what, in peasant societies especially, was a familiar degree of social collectivism. Moreover, even superficial sympathy for communist ideas was sufficient to attract the support of the Soviet Union and its allies, whose assistance, however cynically offered, was often indispensable in military terms.

Communism is a deep chord, especially in Asia, but it is not the main melody across the whole period. The main melody is revolution, in the most elementary sense: war to turn things upside down. Sometimes the targets are Western interests, either directly or as embodied in post-colonial élites deemed to have been corrupted by the patronage of foreigners. At other times, it is the withdrawal or collapse of Western power that leads to war, by allowing traditional animosities to regain their former salience, or by creating a space within which competing revolutionary parties can contend for power.

Radical ends lent themselves to radical means. Wars of national liberation are disproportionately associated with irregular warfare, guerrilla insurgency and terrorism, an important connection that should not be misunderstood. Such methods testify not merely to revolutionary intention, but to military weakness. By themselves they rarely produce decisive results, and they are chosen only by those too weak to advance their claims by conventional means. New or aspiring nations capable of employing regular armies invariably do so. North Korea abandoned a smouldering war of subversion against its southern neighbour once it had assembled an overwhelming preponderance of conventional force.

One of the most important consequences of the chaotic fighting that created the state of Israel in 1948 was the rapid emergence of a highly professional regular army, without which the new nation could not have survived the persisting antagonism of its enemies. Even in cases where irregular warfare plays a more prominent role regular armies are often decisive in the end; though, in truth, firm generalizations remain elusive. Saigon is liberated by tanks, but Algiers and Havana are not. What links the episodes that concern us is less a shared tactical outlook than a common strategic purpose. Always the dominant aim is the violent pursuit of radical political change; war to create or control a national state grounded in some kind of cultural community.

David Ben-Gurion, Israel's first Prime Minister, proclaiming his new state's independence, 14 May 1948. Behind him is a picture of Theodor Herzl (1860–1904), whose writings helped inspire the emigration of European Jews to Palestine.

The formation of nations out of the wreckage of empires is a central theme of world history in the middle decades of the twentieth century. But it is not the only theme, and its weight is not sufficient to allow the construction of a master narrative of decolonization into which each example can be neatly fitted. Collectively, the wars of national liberation lack the operatic structure of the world wars that engendered them. They possess sufficient military and political cohesion to make it worthwhile to think about them together, but it is wrong to minimize or obscure differences. A category encompassing nearly every major armed clash for thirty years following the end of the Second World War is by its nature going to have limited power to explain specific events.

Nevertheless, this volume proceeds on the assumption that the wars it studies inhabit a common historical space that is not shared, for instance, by the triangular struggle that arose among China, Vietnam and Kampuchea (Cambodia) in the late 1970s, or by the Falklands War, or the two wars in the Persian Gulf – all of which are more reminiscent of classic *Realpolitik* than of wars fought to build nations. These conflicts date roughly from the 1980s, which may well be remembered as the decade when the spasms of violence generated by the world wars had sufficiently run their course to enable mankind to resume fighting about other things. Yet the last of the great European empires, that of the Soviet Union, survived until 1989, and it is possible that its collapse will inspire patterns of conflict similar to those discussed here. Indeed, in Afghanistan, Chechnya and elsewhere in Central Asia it may already be doing so, albeit in an international environment reminiscent of the 1920s, in which the intervention of powerful outsiders is largely absent.

How did such wars come about and become so dangerous? The chapters that follow try to provide sensible answers for the most compelling cases; but it is also a question worth some general discussion. The idea that the unravelling of European hegemony would be a violent process was familiar long before the evidence for its truth became apparent. One of the motives that had driven the empire builders in the first place, after all, had been a belief that Western domination would bring peace and order to societies that seemed – sometimes on too superficial acquaintance, sometimes fairly enough – to have little of either. Whether such idealistic impulses could ever have outweighed more preponderant, self-interested concerns with wealth and power is impossible to say. There is in any case no question that Europe's empires were created and sustained by force, and functioned for the benefit of those who wielded it. That their downfall would be attended by violence was less surprising than that it should have happened so quickly, and so soon.

One of the least appreciated aspects of the modern European empires is the brevity of their existence. Although Europeans had been aware of a wider world since medieval times – Marco Polo visited what is now southern Vietnam at the end of the thirteenth century – their period of pre-eminence was remarkably limited. Rome may not have been built in a day, but evanescent structures like the French Indo-Chinese Union might as well have been: when Ho Chi Minh was born it was barely three years old. Even the British position in India had existed for only a century or so before its end had become foreseeable. As early as 1839, a parliamentary commission was prepared to envision the British Empire, not yet at its greatest extent, evolving into a system of self-governing dominions, a process reaffirmed and strengthened by the Statute of Westminster in 1931 which established the British Commonwealth as a system of states freely associating with each other. A sense that the imperial enterprise had not had a fair chance to do its work animated some of those, like Winston Churchill, who pleaded between the wars for policies that would postpone final divestiture, in order to forestall a resurgent tribalism. By then, however, the debate in Britain had boiled down to when, and not whether. On the continent empires were viewed as permanent possessions, whose future evolution would be towards common citizenship with the metropole, combined with whatever elements of local autonomy might add to administrative efficiency.

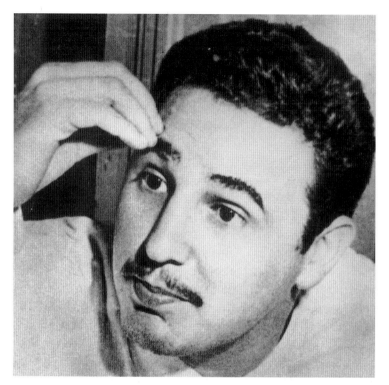

Fidel Castro in 1953, the year of his first attempt to seize power in Cuba. Like most revolutionary leaders, Castro was young, well-educated and came from a middle-class family.

Marxist critics of Western imperialism were quick to recognize that it contained the seeds of its own destruction. It was not easy to anticipate exactly what kinds of blossoms these might produce. Lenin was wrong to imagine that imperialism was simply an elaboration of capitalism, extending the competition among bourgeois states to broader fields, and multiplying opportunities for their interests to clash; wrong, at any rate, to suppose the problems would prove insurmountable by familiar means. The wars that doomed European imperialism did not start in the imperial hinterlands, but in the heart of Europe. Yet Lenin was right to see that the modernizing effects of even brief contact with the West would place new ideological, organizational and military means in the hands of native peoples, without necessarily moderating their resentments. Marxism was itself part of this Western heritage – egalitarian, deeply rationalist, ruthless in its claims on society, and as intolerant of traditional values as the most self-satisfied liberalism. It proved no less serviceable than the new European methods for managing a bureaucracy, collecting taxes, disposing of sewage or delivering the mail.

Despite all premonitions there was much that was surprising about the post-war wars. Advocates of collective security believed changes in the international system would make such conflicts unnecessary, a point of view that found expression in the League of Nations. The League became a halfway house for decolonization in a fit of absence of mind, thanks to the liquidation of the German, Ottoman and Austro-Hungarian empires after 1918. The system of League Mandates created to supervise the transition of subject peoples to independent sovereignty had been devised mainly to protect the interests of the mandatory powers, who had colonies of their own. The main reason it succeeded as far as it did was that most strong countries were prepared to co-operate in preserving international order, and did not seek to exploit unrest at the expense of their rivals.

Nevertheless, the League enshrined national self-determination as a capital political value, and it seemed inevitable that it would spread throughout the world. This expectation was strengthened by the ascendancy of the United States to the leadership of the United Nations, the League's more robust successor. The USA had never flinched from asserting what it regarded as its natural hegemony in the Western Hemisphere. Towards the end of the nineteenth century it even acquired a modest overseas establishment of its own, thanks to its victory in the Spanish–American War. Yet it was also a superb example of a former colony made good, and a perennial critic of European imperialism, if for no other reason than because the US feared its economic and strategic consequences.

This outlook was reinforced by post-war anxieties about the military and political balance in Europe. Americans were disinclined to see any strategic purpose in dispersing Western energy and resources into every corner of the world. This point of view would change along with changing perceptions of the global nature of the communist threat, until, in the end, the US found itself defending the last bastions of a system it had always deprecated. In the meantime, there seemed to be little doubt that the balance of world opinion had shifted against the perpetuation of Western authority where it was no longer wanted.

Other observers, in a harder spirit, were taken by surprise for different reasons. If the recent past proved anything, it was felt, it must be that modern wars escalate uncontrollably. In a world dominated by two irremediably hostile powers, each with global interests and vast military resources, merely regional war seemed not so much unnecessary as inconceivable. Both of the world wars had arisen from quarrels over who should rule in Eastern Europe. Once the shooting started war had engulfed the whole world, twice, despite the fact that the original quarrel had meant little to anyone not directly involved. Even with all the advantages of hindsight it was not easy to see how this could have been avoided, nor how to keep the same sort of thing from happening again. These thoughts drove out serious concern with what the nineteenth century had called 'small wars', to which was added a residual confidence that, should such troubles somehow arise without the sky falling, they would not stretch the capacities of good armies.

The proposition that modern conditions had consigned limited war to the dustbin of history resulted from overestimating the typicality of the recent past. It was an honest mistake, at least in the sense that it had been made before. The first theorist to note the historical preponderance of limited war, Carl von Clausewitz, did so at a time when most experts were convinced that the all-in conflagration of the Napoleonic era represented the perfection of earlier forms of fighting, from which there was no going back. Clausewitz, on the other hand, thought that wars fought to achieve the total defeat of an enemy would always be rare, for reasons arising from war's character as a political instrument, and from the 'friction' that attended its use. War for limited objectives – a province, a concession, an apology, prestige – was the norm, and any strategic posture that failed to take this into account was likely to be discredited in the long run.

It is an insight worth having, though like most important ideas it raises as many questions as it answers. Clausewitz, having analytically subordinated all war to politics – itself, as he says, 'merely the representative of all the interests of the community, taken as a whole' – also said that wars fought with limited means for limited ends were 'more political' than others. It is on its face a logical error, but one that captures an important psychological truth. The routine characterization of conflicts like the Napoleonic wars or the world wars as 'total' should not obscure the fact that even the most all-encompassing clash of arms is conducted within a complex array of social, economic, diplomatic and customary constraints. The military leadership that fought the world wars did not consider itself to be free from the burdens of political oversight. Nevertheless, the Second World War especially had been fought, at least on the Allied side, under conditions that permitted a uniquely fluid convergence of military and political objectives. Unconditional surrender is a form of words that probably makes more sense to a soldier than to a diplomat, and it set a standard for the reconciliation of civil and military interests that would be difficult to recapture in the post-war era, when political ends and military means often seemed hopelessly at odds.

The persistent complaint that Western armies since 1945 have fought for poorly defined goals is misleading if it is taken to mean that military and political objectives should automatically cohere, or that conditions in which they do not are always fraught with disaster. It is rather the case that war and politics, having briefly learned to speak something like the same language in the course of an all-encompassing global conflict, thereafter ceased to do so once the political stakes had shrunk to more normal proportions. More critically, they ceased to do so in a context where the need for adequate means of translation was not always recognized. Here one sees the baleful effect not of ignorance, but of experience. The historical record of Western colonial warfare had been one of such consistent mastery that even the most piddling setbacks – Little Big Horn, Isandhlwana, El Camarón – had become the stuff of legend. When the European empires were being created, tactical success had pretty much spoken for itself.

The point should not be overdrawn. The experiences of empire had provided ample evidence of the need for patience and persistence in combating irregular forces, the importance of controlling, protecting and pacifying the civil population, the vital role of good intelligence, and so on. The West had even produced its share of heroes on the other side of the question. T. E. Lawrence's exploits as leader of the Arab revolt in the First World War were well known to Mao. His German contemporary, Paul von Lettow-Vorbeck, proved equally proficient as an irregular warrior, conducting a guerrilla campaign in East Africa and Mozambique that occupied 100,000 British Imperial troops between 1914 and 1918. Algerian revolutionaries styled themselves *maquis* in mocking tribute to their putative brothers in arms in the French Resistance. Changing technologies aside, the military methods of all sides in the post-war wars were scarcely unprecedented. The only unfamiliar part, at least in some cases, were the results.

Any explanation for the relative success of Third World revolutionary warfare after 1945 must take account of the asymmetrical motives that sometimes drove the antagonists. Not all parties to the wars of national liberation counted the costs the same way, and those that counted them most closely often felt themselves at a psychological disadvantage that material superiority could not offset. Such considerations obviously apply only in circumstances where the limited interests of one side are apparent. It would be fatuous to characterize the outcome of the fighting between Chinese Communists and Nationalists, or between the Jews and Arabs in Palestine, as mere failures of nerve. The major defeats of Western forces in our period, however – especially of France in Indo-China and Algeria, and of the United States in Vietnam – are commonly viewed in precisely this light, and it is worth emphasizing that this is less illuminating than it may seem. The easy Western triumphs of earlier times had been accomplished despite an identical disadvantage: there has never been a moment since the European Age of Discovery when the fate of Indo-China did not matter more to the people of Hué than to those of Paris, much less New York. In the old days, however, this sort of asymmetry made no difference. A passionate desire for freedom counts for little if it cannot be translated into effective military, political and diplomatic strategies. It is because the non-European world had learned to employ such strategies, not least by virtue of contact with the West, that the conflicts attending the dissolution of European empires proved so different from those that created them.

Two features stand out across the whole period. The first is the ability of revolutionary movements to appeal to the interests and sympathy of outsiders without spoiling their claim to be champions of national identity. This amounts in the simplest terms to the skilful pursuit of international aid, ranging from economic and diplomatic support to direct military intervention. Although such assistance does not guarantee success, its absence is virtually synonymous with failure. More broadly, one sees a new appreciation of the importance of global opinion as an element of the international system. From the start, the far-flung commitments of Western nations had rested on contested moral ground, and depended upon a process of continuous compromise and the adjustment of competing interests among the colonizers. In the middle decades of the twentieth century this uncertain dynamic, and the limited nature of the military and political measures it was capable of supporting, became fully visible to everyone, and consequently subject to attack by methods that extended far beyond what is normally meant by 'propaganda'. The wars of national liberation include many military actions calculated to appeal directly to the ideals or anxieties of civil society on the other side, or to neutral outsiders who might impose a sense of proportion upon one's enemy. The atavistic violence or tactical futility that sometimes marked such operations, as judged by conventional standards, did not necessarily lessen their political effects.

The second distinguishing feature is a new capacity to bear the burdens of protracted war. This, again, is not simply a matter of will-power, but of new capacities for organization, stemming from the resiliency of the national idea itself. Nations are social constructions, erected in defiance of the real historical experience of traditional societies, in which the dissipation of political authority through

The first meeting of the United Nations Security Council, 29 March 1946. At that time, the UN had fifty members. By the end of 1999 it had 188.

elaborate forms of social deference is a pre-eminent theme. Nationalism elevates the claims of ethnicity, language and religion above fragmentary structures of tribe, caste and clan. In a Third World context, it also trades upon the shared experience of foreign rule. Modern empires are tributes to the power of the nation state, and it is not surprising that those subjected to them would acquire a lively appreciation of this fact. By refocusing political loyalty upon the state – even in embryonic form as revolutionary movement or party – the spread of nationalism around the world created military possibilities that were not available to the provincial native élites that confronted the original expansion of Western influence.

Seizing those possibilities is by no means easy. The task, after all, is to mobilize the nation not in self-defence but in self-creation. Wars of national liberation are frequently represented as episodes of spontaneous combustion produced by pervasive misery and injustice: war as the product of revolution. Yet the opposite dynamic is equally apparent: revolution as a product of war, waged by a committed vanguard whose outlook does not command widespread support at the start, and who may obtain only grudging acquiescence even at the end. Nothing is more common than putatively revolutionary movements that identify themselves with the nation but fail to mature politically, sometimes fading away after a few violent episodes, sometimes persisting for years on the margins of the societies they hoped to transform. The line between political action and banditry, as Mao might have said, is one that mere persistence cannot erase.

Time, in any case, is a neutral factor in war. Or, more precisely, it favours the side that makes the best use of it. The protracted nature of revolutionary war is partly a function of limited military resources, which may reflect material weakness, or the impact of non-military constraints on one side or the other. Such factors make themselves felt regardless of the tactical methods employed. Even the Arab–Israeli wars, which appear on their face to be textbook demonstrations of speed and decisiveness, only make sense if they are understood as elements of a continuous conflict spanning decades. The briefest (and most conventional) of the major wars that concern us here, in Korea, lasted three years, a long time if one considers that more than half of all casualties in the war were suffered after negotiations to end it had begun. The same is true of the American war in Vietnam.

Protracted conflict in our period also reflects the emergence of military methods that embrace the passage of time as a positive element. Guerrilla insurgency, the paradigmatic tactic of revolutionary war, is by definition a method for waging protracted war, in which a limited capacity for violence is applied not to achieve military success, but to delegitimize the government, indoctrinate or demoralize the population and build a political structure capable, in the fullness of time, of taking over. Because the insurgent does not seek a rapid victory, he often proves highly resistant to measures intended to impose rapid defeat, the normal goal of conventional military operations. Successful counter-insurgency in turn succeeds not by cutting short the time available for political action but by employing that time more effectively than the adversary. On both sides the challenge is the same: how to harmonize military and political effort. For the revolutionary this typically resolves itself into the question of when to expose political capital to the risks of battle. For his opponents, it tends to involve moderating large-scale combat operations in favour of methods more conducive to social or political reform.

The course and outcome of the wars of national liberation are shaped by such decisions; which is another way of saying that, despite the atmosphere of inevitability that overhangs them, the post-war wars are contingent events, the outcomes of which were finally decided not by the undeniably profound causes that produced them, but by the skill and determination with which they were fought. Collectively, they represent the birth throes of a radically new world system, comprised entirely of sovereign states controlled by the people who live in them. Whether such a system can endure, or what it may in turn become, is beyond anyone's ken. In any case, its violent origins will repay careful study.

CHAPTER ONE

China

Chinese Communist troops march in Beijing, June 1949. The city had fallen six months before. Parades of this kind were supposed to stimulate enthusiasm for the new regime and its leader, Mao Tse-tung, whose image is born aloft on the truck at the centre of the crowd.

China

In an epoch in which imperialism exists, a genuine people's revolution cannot win victory in any country without help from the international revolutionary forces.

Mao Tse-tung, speech of 30 June 1949

THE WAR THAT brought the Chinese Communists to power in 1949 was the culmination of a series of conflicts that followed the fall of the Qing dynasty in 1912, an event that had previously claimed the title 'Chinese revolution'. A pseudo-republican regime followed, under the presidency of military strongman Yuan Shikai, whose Paiyang Army was the most modern fighting force in a country that had been teetering towards civil war since the turn of the century. Yuan's death in 1916 gave rise to a renewed contest for power, which this time produced no clear winner. By 1919 China had ceased, for practical purposes, to be a unified country, having fallen under the sway of provincial 'warlords' whose intramural quarrels dominated the 1920s. The warlords would in turn be suppressed by the Kuomintang (KMT), a nationalist party whose leading figure, Sun Yat-sen, served briefly as China's provisional president before being ousted by Yuan. The KMT's efforts were supported for a time by the Chinese Communist Party (CCP), founded in 1921 as an outpost of Lenin's Third International, and also directly by the new Soviet Union, which recognized the revolutionary opportunity that China's decrepitude afforded, and also that the expulsion of Western influence from Asia was in its interest. Both the KMT and the CCP were revolutionary and anti-imperialist movements intent upon governing a unified China, and this shared aspiration made co-operation against common enemies possible – first the warlords and later the Japanese. Once the latter had been beaten, however, a final showdown became unavoidable. At the end the Communists controlled all of China except Taiwan, to which the KMT retired once its position on the mainland had become hopeless.

The roots of this complex struggle can be traced to the entanglement of the two main protagonists in the 1920s. Between them, the Kuomintang was by far the stronger, being descended from a long line of reformist and anti-Western associations extending back to the 1890s. Such sentiments were amplified by the First World War. Japan, bound to the Entente by virtue of its 1902 alliance with Great Britain, seized Germany's holdings around Shandong, and sought to use this foothold to extract concessions not unlike those that had brought war with China twenty years before. No Western power was prepared to restrain Japan, even after China entered the war at America's behest. At the same time, the war reduced Western economic activity in China, which afforded new scope for native commercial and social initiatives. A movement of modernizing cultural criticism arose, based upon Western ideas of democratic individualism and scientific learning, and directed simultaneously against traditional Confucian practices, persisting

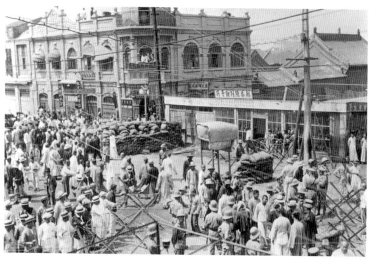

The warlords brought modern war to China, and the KMT rose amid the social chaos and political weakness that resulted. Shown here are the streets of Tiensin in 1924, blocked by military barbed wire and sandbag machine-gun emplacements – both relative novelties at the time.

Western influence and the encroaching Japanese. It acquired a name – the May Fourth Movement – following a violent mass protest against the terms of the Versailles Treaty, by which Japan would be allowed to retain the former German leaseholds it had seized during the war.

The May Fourth Movement created an atmosphere that favoured the KMT's programme of national regeneration. It also provided the early leadership for the Chinese Communist Party, whose growth was made easier by Western complacency. While the victors of 1918 were eager to reassert their rights under the 'unequal treaties' negotiated in the nineteenth century, Lenin's government declared itself willing to renounce the concessions won by the tsars at China's expense – a reflection of weakness rather than generosity, but symbolically impressive just the same. The Comintern agents sent to China in the spring of 1920 received a cordial welcome, both from activists drawn to communism as such, and from the KMT leadership. When early efforts to create an independent communist movement based on factory workers and the railway unions faltered, the CCP's focus shifted to infiltrating its revolutionary rival. Sun, who did not foresee that the rivalry would one day prove mortal, accepted communists into the KMT as individual members. He also relied on Soviet advice in reorganizing the KMT's party structure, and in consolidating its authority in Guangdong, a province remote from the centres of power, on China's southern coast.

China, like France, is a country best conquered from the north. It was from there that the Manchus had come in the seventeenth century, and it was also there, and around Shanghai, that the most serious local wars occurred in the 1920s. It is not possible here even to summarize the course of these clashes, which can be conceived as something like a round robin tournament, in which weaker contestants were absorbed by the increasingly exhausted winners. Sun, dependent at first upon the mercenary armies of southern warlords, dreamt of a Northern Expedition to cut the Gordian knot of provincial militarism, but did not live to see it. That task would fall to his protégé, Chiang Kai-shek,

The May Thirtieth movement galvanized political unrest throughout China. The picture shows a student demonstration in Canton in November 1925, demanding an end to the unequal treaties that afforded foreigners special economic, social and legal rights.

who assumed effective leadership of the Kuomintang following Sun's death in March 1925.

Chiang was a military man. In contrast to Sun, whose personal outlook had drifted to the left during his years of reliance upon the Soviet Union, Chiang was wary of communists within the KMT. He was also determined to employ his well-trained, Soviet-style forces to some useful purpose. Events favoured him. On 30 May 1925, a demonstration in Shanghai, called to protest the killing of a Chinese worker by a Japanese factory guard, broke down in bloody violence after British police fired into a crowd that seemed about to rush their station. Such scenes were scarcely unprecedented in China, or for that matter in Shanghai. This time, however, the usual waves of civil unrest that followed failed to subside – testimony to the general weakening of the social fabric wrought by the internecine struggles of the last five years. By mid summer, boycotts, strikes and assorted mayhem – collectively remembered as the May Thirtieth Movement – had spread throughout China, often under the leadership of CCP cadres in the cities. Yet it was the Kuomintang whose hour had struck. Its promise to renounce the unequal treaties and restore national authority resonated strongly within the institutional and psychological vacuum the warlords had created. Most crucially, the KMT possessed a military force capable of enforcing its claims. While the CCP was fomenting revolution, Chiang would make war.

Chiang launched his newly christened National Revolutionary Army (NRA) north from Guangdong in July 1926. Although inferior to its numerous opponents in numbers, superior training, equipment and morale made up the difference. Progress was rapid, but in some respects illusory, since it was often achieved by inducing enemy commanders to bring their troops over to the KMT side, a move that allowed them to preserve much of their old autonomy in a new, revolutionary guise. Most NRA divisions had Soviet advisers, and auxiliary units devoted to propaganda and subversion. The latter could be a double-edged sword. Areas brought under Nationalist control became subject to radicalizing measures organized by operatives left behind in the army's wake. The CCP leadership was divided as to how far it should seek to exploit such opportunities. Mao Tse-tung, assigned by the party to investigate unrest in rural Hunan, reported that the peasant masses were the only revolutionary base available; that their revolutionary consciousness was all that theory demanded; and that their incipient revolt should be encouraged. A majority, however, continued to favour a strategy based on the proletariat, and hoped to preserve the link with the Kuomintang, agent of the bourgeois revolution that would perforce precede their own.

Disappointment awaited them. With the fall of Nanjing and Shanghai in March 1927, Chiang felt able to dispense with his Communist partners, whose conduct had become alarming to the propertied groups at the heart of the KMT's social base. A vicious purge ensued, in which thousands died. The CCP fought back. On 1 August army units sympathetic to the Communists briefly seized the town of Nanchang, an action later memorialized as the founding date of the People's Liberation Army, but disastrous at the time. Mao organized an uprising dubbed 'Autumn Harvest' in rural Hunan. A white terror by landlords and village militias crushed it. In December, an insurrection in Canton was suppressed with terrible losses. By the end of the year, forces loyal to the CCP had been reduced to a few scattered bands, which eventually coalesced in the hard country of Hunan and Jiangxi. Mao, having been among the first to recognize that the way forward ran through the countryside, would later emerge as their natural leader.

Chiang, having thus dealt with the Communist threat, resumed his campaign against the northern warlords. Beijing fell in June 1928, and in October a new national government was proclaimed in Nanjing. It immediately obtained international recognition. With it came financial and military resources, by which residual warlordism was further reduced. Hard fighting ended in June 1930, when the last major anti-Chiang faction was suppressed. In practice, Chiang's writ did not run much beyond the cities and transportation corridors of eastern China. His personal position was likewise circumscribed by the endless intrigues that afflicted the KMT. This was a problem that arose partly from military practices, specifically the direct co-optation of provincial warlords into the NRA itself. In years to come, many an opportunity for decisive success would be squandered by subordinates resentful of Chiang's authority, commanding what were still semi-private armies. Yet few observers doubted, at the end of 1930, that the decade-long round robin for national leadership had finally produced a winner.

It remained to root the Communists out of their mountain fastness. This was not a task to capture Chiang's imagination. He was preoccupied with looming conflict with Japan, which retained important, but in its view inadequate, privileges in Manchuria. The NRA's best troops were reserved to counter this threat. In October, however, Chiang dispatched an army of former warlord troops against newly proclaimed soviets in Oyuwan and Jiangxi, in a campaign of 'encirclement and extermination'. Neither was achieved. The soldiers sent to fight the Communists were poorly trained, and were led by commanders who lacked any compelling motive to consume their own forces by engaging Chiang's enemies. Moreover, the operation did not aim at envelopment, but sought to sweep the Communists out of their hiding places like the bandits they were imagined to be. In such a contest, mobility and good local intelligence are essential. Both favoured the Communists, who fought a war of feints and ambushes that rapidly demoralized their opponents.

A second campaign in the spring of 1931 fared little better, though it was based on a more promising concept, with multiple columns advancing concentrically towards a common centre. Execution, however, was still hampered by commanders reluctant to risk casualties, and by poor co-ordination among detached forces. No solid front was achieved, and two NRA divisions were trapped and broken by infiltrating Communist counter-attacks. In the end, the first two encirclement campaigns left the Communists stronger, more confident, and, thanks to captured *matériel*, better equipped than they had been at the start.

In July, Chiang decided to commit his best troops and commanders to the struggle. This made a genuinely dangerous scheme of manoeuvre possible. The target was the Jiangxi Soviet, where about 55,000 troops were concentrated under Chu Teh, the man destined to lead the Red forces to victory in 1949. The plan was for NRA forces to establish a blocking line on the Kan River, against which the enemy would be driven by forces converging from the north-east. The threat posed by this operation can be judged by the Communist response: a scorched earth retreat extending hundreds of miles, featuring the wholesale destruction of local food supplies, the poisoning of wells, and the forcible evacuation of civilians. Such actions slowed the KMT advance, but at appreciable cost to the CCP's hold on the loyalty of the population. In August, the main Communist force tried to break out by storming the town of Huang Po, and got badly shot up. About half later escaped thanks to a surprise night march through a narrow gap in the NRA lines. But even these might have been pursued had not external events supervened.

In September 1931, the officers of Japan's Kwangtung Army, deployed in Manchuria to protect the Japanese leasehold on the Liaotung Peninsula and along the South Manchurian Railway, began moving their forces south, on the pretext of expelling the local warlord they had previously supported. This initiative was designed to commit the Japanese government to an expansionist policy it had not approved, but towards which it was now inexorably drawn. It also forced Chiang to break off his campaign in Jiangxi. It was not until May 1932 that a truce was arranged, by which Japan's de facto possession of Manchuria was ratified; and not until January that Chiang's forces could again turn against the Communists. A second pause was required in March after Japanese forces struck below the Great Wall into Jehol, an action that forced Chiang's government to concede the establishment of a demilitarized zone on Chinese territory in the north. It was a

Japanese forces in Jehol, 1933. The rapid expansion and collapse of Japanese military power was crucial to the emergence of national liberation movements throughout Asia. Yet Japan itself was scarcely a rich or powerful country at the time, merely a determined and opportunistic one.

dangerous pattern. In the eyes of his critics, Chiang's appeasement of the Japanese in order to pursue the Communists suggested something between confusion and betrayal. In fact, his priorities conformed to the military facts: Chiang could not do much about the Japanese in Manchuria. He could about the Communists in Jiangxi.

In October he struck them again, deploying 750,000 troops in a methodical campaign to reduce the entirety of the Communists' southern base. In tactical terms, the key problem had always been to control the superior mobility that had allowed Red forces to elude destruction. This would now be solved by means of a network of concrete blockhouses, built at narrow intervals along major lines of communication throughout Jiangxi. New roads and telegraph lines were also laid down, to allow co-ordinated movement on the Nationalist side. The civil population was finally mobilized against the Reds, partly because their labour was required for the new construction, but also because, as Chiang had said, the problem of dealing with the Communists was only 30 per cent military, and 70 per cent political.

The NRA's blockhouses presented a serious obstacle to an adversary that lacked weapons heavy enough to reduce them. Having subdivided the terrain by means of these modest fortifications, each segmented area was then flooded with troops, many of whose officers had now been given special training in irregular warfare – an indirect benefit of the pause imposed by Japanese pressure in the north. The Communists also adopted new methods. Unwilling to face the consequences of another wholesale retreat, the Red forces, on the advice of Soviet experts, chose to fight a positional campaign along the perimeter of their base. They leaned into the punch. By the summer of 1934 it had become clear that the Jiangxi Soviet could not be held. 15,000 soldiers and about 20,000 political operatives were detailed to remain behind as a kind of rearguard, among them Mao's brother and two children by his third wife, all of whom perished. The rest fought their way out, breaking through in sectors whose commanders, rivals of Chiang within the KMT, had disdained to build the blockhouse cordon meant to contain them.

Thus commenced one of the epic retreats of modern war. The Long March is universally recognized as a defining moment of Chinese history. Few events are better suited to become the stuff of myth, though precisely for that reason the details are difficult to reconstruct. About 100,000 troops broke out of Jiangxi, intending to regroup in northern Hunan with Red forces fleeing Oyuwan. This number was rapidly reduced by the desertion of troops from the surrounding area, who were reluctant to abandon their native region. Thus diminished, the Jiangxi columns moved south and west to avoid superior Nationalist forces in their path. Perhaps 30,000 remained when Tunyi was taken in January. Of these, as few as one in three may have survived the trek to Yenan, a reflection of the legendary hardships of the journey, rather than of the half-hearted pursuit by their enemies. Although the march through thousands of miles of western China would later be represented as a campaign of political mobilization, the reality was different. Deprived of their base, Communist forces found only grudging support from the peasant communities through which they passed. Much had been lost. Two years earlier, Red troops and political cadres controlled areas with a total population of about 50 million. All that would have to be rebuilt. If Napoleon, limping back from Moscow with little more than the Guard for company, had gone on to conquer Europe anyway, it would not have been more surprising.

It was the Long March that finally secured Mao's ascendancy over the communist movement in China. None of the advocates of the CCP's original strategy of urban insurrection survived, and the Soviet advisers who had conceived the conventional defence of Jiangxi had been discredited by the results. The Long March also provided him, in somewhat Darwinian fashion, with a hard core of followers ready to support his strategy for rural insurgency.

That strategy is usually summarized as describing a revolutionary war of three phases. In the first, defensive phase, the emphasis falls upon indoctrination of the civil population, and the development of party cadres capable of engaging in isolated acts of violence – sabotage, assassination, ambush, and so on – intended to undermine the credibility of the established regime. Once this process has sufficiently progressed, a second phase is entered, signified by the establishment of secure territorial bases, from which organized forces approaching conventional size may operate, seeking always to concentrate superior numbers against isolated enemy units, to preserve mobility by timely retreat, and so on. The final stage arises when the physical and psychological attrition achieved by such attacks has sufficiently shifted the balance to allow large-scale operations against the centres of government power – a transformation, Mao knew, that might require outside assistance.

In operational terms, Mao's ideas do not differ from the kinds of conclusions that anyone familiar with the long history of irregular warfare might have reached. Nor should their formulaic quality be overestimated. The idea that revolutionary insurgency unfolds in three discrete, sequential stages is more a product of Western counter-insurgency doctrine than it is of Mao's writings, which are more concerned with mastering his own situation than with providing a generic recipe for success. His ideas are distinctive, from the point of view of the Marxist tradition, chiefly in their identification of the peasantry as a revolutionary class – an insight anticipated by Lenin, but still suspect, as we have seen, within the Soviet military establishment, on whose advice the Chinese Communists, and others around the world, had previously relied.

More generally, Mao's work put new flesh on the bones of Clausewitz's familiar proposition that war is a political instrument. Clausewitz's work had always held a special attraction for revolutionaries. Friedrich Engels, a military expert, had been among the first to recognize its importance. Lenin, languishing in his Swiss exile, had copied and annotated long passages from *On War* in a notebook that later become the bible of Bolshevik military theory, reproduced in editions running into the hundreds of thousands in the 1920s and 30s. In Mao's work, however, the political nature of war achieved a new depth of tactical articulation. While Clausewitz believed, as he says, that politics will not determine the posting of guards, Mao was not so sure. He recognized that grassroots social action – harvesting crops, running off bandits, promoting literacy, building dykes and bridges – was the indispensable complement to small-scale military violence, because it allowed the revolutionary warrior to occupy the political and psychological void his own actions were intended to create. To this end, the personal conduct of Red cadre was also rigidly prescribed, to contrast as sharply as possible with the peremptory behaviour of regular soldiers. Real revolutionaries, Mao insisted, pay for their meals and make their beds. Much romance attaches to such ideas, but it should not. Brutality towards recalcitrant civilians was also part of the Maoist method. The revolutionary fish swimming in the sea of the people was, in real life, a piranha.

The question facing the survivors of the Long March was whether basically familiar methods of guerrilla warfare, even if waged in the most politically sophisticated fashion, could produce decisive results against a foe that had apparently learned how to defeat them. In theoretical terms, Mao's analysis of revolutionary insurgency was more in the nature of a hope than an inference. His embrace of the virtues of protracted struggle was not unlike the confidence a psychiatrist feels about his ability to cure a patient, despite lingering doubts as to whether it can be done in this lifetime. For this dilemma, Mao had only his adversary to blame. In the years since the break-up of the KMT–CCP united front against the warlords, the balance of strategic advantage had shifted towards the Nationalists. There was nothing about the new base at Yenan that ruled out a continuation of the encirclement campaigns. It had become the party's refuge mainly because it lay across the frontier from the Mongolian People's Republic, a Soviet client state that would afford a final sanctuary if the Nationalist offensive was renewed.

It was not. As has been seen, Chiang's determination to liquidate the Communists was not universal within the Kuomintang. The shift of the Red base to the north heightened the problem, because it meant that a sixth campaign would have to be conducted by commands deployed opposite the Japanese. Chiang's efforts to compel their co-operation failed. In December 1936, on a journey to extract a promise of action against Yenan from one of them, Chiang was briefly taken hostage by his own men, and forced to accept a new united front. Japan, fearing that the KMT's accommodation with the CCP presaged a Sino-Soviet alliance, became even more anxious about its position in Manchuria. In July, following a minor clash between Japanese and Chinese troops at the Marco Polo Bridge in Beijing, Chiang moved NRA troops into the demilitarized zone near the city. Japan announced a deadline for their removal, then attacked anyway. By mid August, fifty Chinese divisions were engaged against a Japanese force of 300,000 at Shanghai. The Second World War in Asia had begun.

The details of its course lie beyond the scope of this volume. Nevertheless, a summary of its impact on the two contestants for power in China is important to an understanding of the revolutionary climax that followed. For the CCP, the united front with the Nationalists required the curtailment of open class warfare, particularly the forcible redistribution of land as a means of recruiting smallholders and tenants in the countryside. Its forbearance was more than made up for by the opportunity to present itself not as a self-interested faction, but as a champion of the whole nation against foreign aggression. Although the Red Army fared no better than their Nationalist counterparts in conventional clashes with the Japanese, its mastery of guerrilla warfare against isolated garrisons contrasted with the dismal record of Nationalist forces incapable of employing such tactics. Although the military results of these operations were inconsequential that did not diminish their political effect. The Japanese never regarded Communist forces as the main threat. They responded to the Red insurgency with just the sort of casual brutality best suited to heighten its moral impact on the civil population.

Chinese citizens search the ruins following a Japanese raid on Hankow, 1938. Although strategic bombing of civil populations began during the First World War, Japanese air attacks, like those of the Luftwaffe in Spain, shocked world opinion. As the Second World War unfolded such methods would become routine for all belligerents.

Small Red units were able to operate for long periods behind Japanese lines, spreading the party's message far beyond their base in Yenan. These campaigns were possible because of the overextended nature of the Japanese position. The Second World War in China was marked by two periods of intense combat: during the main Japanese advance from 1937 to 1939, and again after May 1944, when the Japanese mounted an offensive into southern China, intended to compensate for the destruction of Japanese merchant marine by establishing continuous rail communications between Manchuria and Indo-China. Although any map portraying conditions in the years in between will show Japanese forces in control of all of north-east and central China, most Japanese troops during this period were deployed in Manchuria, to watch the Soviets, or opposite the Nationalist forces driven south by the initial Japanese surge. In the middle lay a vast, semi-occupied region where the basic structures of KMT authority had been destroyed, but not replaced. The CCP's proficiency in filling this vacuum – far more extensive than any it could have created by its own strength – was vital to its subsequent success. In the spring of 1945, the party claimed to dispose of regular and militia forces numbering 3 million, and to control areas with a population of 90 million. However exaggerated such figures might be, there can be no question that the war against Japan led to a dramatic expansion in Communist influence and prestige.

It bled the Kuomintang. NRA forces bore the brunt of conventional fighting during the two periods when it was most intense. Losses in the early years of the war proved especially critical, because they included a large share of the professional officer corps whose creation had been one of the party's most important achievements. In contrast to the CCP, the KMT found no means of profiting from Japanese passivity during the war's middle years. Driven off its base along China's eastern seaboard and in the lower Yangtze River valley, Chiang's government was deprived of its most important sources of revenue, which derived from maritime trade. Its besetting sins – corruption and bureaucratization – were accordingly amplified by rampant

CHINA IN THE
SECOND WORLD WAR 1937–45
The 'China Incident' remains the least well known of the great struggles that combined to create the Second World War. Chinese armies suffered at least 3 million casualties fighting the Japanese. Civilian losses are unknown, but certainly many times greater.

China in the
Second World War 1937–45

▨	under Japanese control 1933
▨	under Communist control from 1935–6
➡	Japanese advances to 1941
▨	under Japanese control by end of 1941
➡	Japanese advance to December 1944
▨	under Japanese control December 1944
▨	under Japanese control 15 August 1945

inflation. By 1945, Chinese currency had lost 98 per cent of its value relative to the American dollar, a demoralizing experience for precisely those groups upon which the KMT relied most heavily for support. American aid, which became available after 1941, was sufficient to keep

China in the war, but not to redress the damage to the KMT's position that the Japanese inflicted.

Nevertheless, when Japan surrendered the Kuomintang was the legitimate government of China in the eyes of the whole world. It had an army twice as large as that of its Communist partners, and was far better equipped with modern weapons. No one, including the CCP leadership, seems to have imagined that the Nationalists' hold on power was about to unravel. It did so as much because of the way the war ended as because of the way it was fought.

In August 1945, Soviet forces invaded Manchuria pursuant to the Yalta Agreement, whereby the USSR would enter the war against Japan three months after fighting ended in Europe. Their immediate aim was to expropriate the industrial plant of one of China's most developed provinces, half of which was packed up and taken away. They also helped restore the KMT administration in Manchurian cities, as Nationalist troops and officials were flown in on American planes. Nevertheless, the Soviet occupation was a boon to the Chinese Communists, who had begun operations to cut off China's northernmost province during the final months of the war. Some 20,000 political cadres, including twenty politburo members, and 100,000 Red troops under the able Lin Piao, were moved into Manchuria with Soviet assistance. Japanese forces elsewhere in China were ordered by the American Supreme Commander, Douglas MacArthur, to surrender only to Nationalist troops. In Manchuria, however, Communist forces under Soviet protection took possession of Japanese arms sufficient to equip 600,000 men.

Nevertheless, they did not prepare for an immediate renewal of war with the Nationalists. Secure behind the occupying Soviet Army they set about consolidating their political position. As in 1927, however, they misjudged their man. In November 1945, even as talks to establish what the Communists hoped would be a coalition government were under way, Chiang threw his best troops into Manchuria, where they soon gained control of the cities and transportation corridors. The Soviet Union, exhausted and wary of conflict with the United States, did not

*Chinese Nationalist troops firing from an improvised trench near Szepinkai,
Manchuria, May 1946. Their targets are their erstwhile Red Army allies. Their
equipment is American, a fact that comported ill with US efforts to broker a
settlement between the two sides.*

intervene. Although the Yalta Agreement that justified the Soviet move
into Manchuria had affirmed their military and administrative primacy
there, they now agreed to Chiang's demand that they withdraw – though
they continued to facilitate CCP infiltration as they did so.

The United States believed that only a negotiated settlement could
prevent total collapse in China. George Marshall, recently retired as
Chief of Staff of the US Army, arrived in December to broker a deal, a
task made more difficult by the fact that American supplies were
fuelling Chiang's Manchurian campaign. Marshall was convinced that
the Communists were too strong to be defeated rapidly, and that
anything else would play into their hands. Albert Wiedemeyer, the
senior American military adviser to Chiang's forces, had argued against
the NRA's offensive into Manchuria on the grounds that it dissipated
resources in a theatre with insurmountable logistical difficulties.
Manchuria, an area three times the size of France, possessed modern
communications only within a thousand-mile rail corridor linking
Beijing and Harbin. In May 1946, with Communist casualties
approaching 50 per cent of their total force, Marshall persuaded

Chiang to halt his advance to avoid further escalation. A pause of some weeks followed. Red forces regrouped, and NRA momentum flagged. American fears about the fragility of NRA logistics were proven correct, as mobile operations gave way to static deployments intended to protect communications with the south.

The strategic significance of these events has been much disputed. Some have held that, by preventing Chiang from ejecting the Reds from Manchuria before they could get their feet under them, the United States threw away the best chance for a Nationalist victory. This analysis turns upon Manchuria's unique characteristic as a base for Red forces: it is the one part of China where a renewed encirclement campaign would have been impossible, owing to the secure flanks afforded by the sea and the Soviet and Korean frontiers, not to mention the parlous communications that so concerned Chiang's American advisers. If Communist forces could have been dug out of this sanctuary right at the start, as Chiang intended, their comrades elsewhere would eventually have become prey to a proven strategy of sequential envelopment and piecemeal annihilation, against which their means of self-defence had not improved.

There is something to be said for this view. Those who reject it

THE CHINESE CIVIL WAR
1945–50
Revolutionary war in China combined subversion and irregular warfare with operations by regular forces numbering in the hundreds of thousands. It was in all its forms a war of infantry, in which heavy weapons, motorized transport and military aircraft were scarce.

Chinese Civil War
1945–50

areas of Communist control

1945–6

1947–8

1949–50

advance by Russian forces

advance by Communist forces

Nationalist attack 1947

withdrawal of Nationalist government to Taiwan

Nationalist territory 1950

BURMA
1947–8: Independent

do so mainly because they doubt its final claim: that the Communists' capacity to withstand operations like those that defeated them in the 1930s did not improve as a consequence of the world war. Thus it is argued that, even if Manchuria had somehow been reduced in 1946 – no sure thing, but easier than at any time thereafter – important

Chinese forces still operated throughout much of the rest of China on a more secure social base than ever before: the political and cultural prestige of the party had been enhanced by its performance in the war, while the material, financial and moral resources of the KMT had been diminished. Whether these advantages would have sufficed for a Red victory without the Manchurian base is impossible to judge, since it involves events that did not occur: Manchuria was in fact the key to the Red victory three years later. In any case, the question should not be allowed to obscure the means by which that victory was actually achieved. The last act of China's long revolution was neither a spontaneous nor even a brilliantly orchestrated explosion of popular violence, but a series of largely conventional and, on the Red side, highly professional military campaigns, in which the strategic initiative shifted steadily towards the Communists.

When George Marshall left China in January 1947 one might easily have imagined that the Nationalists were the main beneficiaries of the slackening pace imposed by America's intervention. Chiang's forces, 5 million strong, were by then deployed in a cordon across all of northern

The Chinese Communists under Mao always depended on the support of the peasantry, to whom they appealed with promises of land reform and social justice generally. The fruits of this policy are shown here, as a train of farmers' carts hauls supplies to Red forces during the Civil War.

China, designed to seal off Red forces in Manchuria, while serving as a base from which to attack the CCP's traditional stronghold in the north-west. Gains so far had been impressive: 165 Communist-held towns and cities fell to NRA forces in the second half of 1946. In March, the Communist capital of Yenan fell, having been left undefended by the party leadership. It was a blow delivered into thin air. Somehow the thread had been lost. Chiang had been quick to grasp the critical importance of the Manchurian theatre. Now that Red forces had got their wind back, however, his operations became diffuse and reactive, as the NRA confronted multiple Red offensives against its communications, mounted from behind the old Japanese lines in central and eastern China.

The superior firepower of Chiang's American-equipped forces continued to count at the tactical level. Major clashes generally went the NRA's way, though at increasing cost as the Reds acquired heavy weapons of their own. Four hundred thousand NRA regulars were killed or captured in 1947. The Red Army undoubtedly suffered worse. But it was better able to make up the losses, thanks to the resumption of land reform in areas under Communist control, which understandably attracted the loyalty of the rural poor. An appreciable number of new recruits came from the NRA itself. Chiang's army, like Mao's, consisted overwhelmingly of peasants. Between 1945 and 1949, 800,000 of them changed sides. Deteriorating economic conditions and endemic corruption within the KMT civil administration contributed to the erosion. Inflation, rampant during the war with Japan, accelerated afterwards, rendering the soldiers' pay worthless, when it appeared at all. By the start of 1948, the NRA's effort to maintain a continuous position in the north had broken down. At the same time, the number of men at its disposal had reached rough parity with the enemy.

The decision now followed swiftly, achieved by well co-ordinated mobile operations across distances similar to those of the Russian campaigns of 1941–4. In December 1947, Lin Piao's 4th Field Army, comprising 600,000 men, attacked the NRA garrisons in Manchuria. Within three months the Nationalists, outnumbered two to one, had been driven into isolated hedgehog positions at Mukden and Changchun. These were sealed off by Red forces moving south against the NRA logistical base at Chingchow. It fell in mid October, along with Changchun, both as a consequence of mutiny among the defenders. Mukden was overrun two weeks later. In September, a second major thrust by the 3rd Field Army under Ch'en Yi pushed east from Shensi into Shantung, crushing NRA forces and driving the remnants south towards the line of the Huai River. Chiang succeeded in concentrating over half a million men at Hsuchow, but the position was immediately broken when four divisions in the centre of the NRA line defected to the enemy. Two hard-fought encirclement battles against the now isolated wings followed. At the end, Chiang ordered his air force, which had been unopposed throughout the fight, to bomb his own armoured formations, lest the equipment fall into Communist hands.

By the start of 1949, nearly all of China north of the Yangtze River was under Communist control. Strong NRA forces remained only around Beijing and Tientsin. These were overwhelmed at the end of January by Lin Piao's forces coming down from Manchuria. An attempt by the KMT to negotiate a partition agreement was brushed aside by Mao. A document of surrender was rejected by the KMT. In April, strong Red forces pushed south against token resistance. Improbably, international assistance appeared in the form of four British warships sent to protect foreign interests in the Yangtze valley. These were run off. The People's Republic of China was proclaimed in October. Chiang and the KMT, along with the Chinese Navy, Air Force and gold reserves, fetched up at Taipei.

Thus ended one of the central military episodes of the twentieth century. Despite the complexity with which events sometimes unfolded, it is not difficult to identify the basic factors that determined the outcome. Chiang's triumph over the warlords was never complete. Military separatism lamed the NRA in the 1930s, and persisted thereafter. Militarily and politically the KMT was a patchwork of barely suppressed rivalries, stitched together by graft – a characteristic expedient of weak governments in poor countries, and not necessarily fatal; yet a serious weakness against an opponent able to make a show of moral rectitude. The world war hurt the KMT worse than its enemy. Its most serious effects were probably economic. War with Japan ruined the economy of those parts of China where money mattered – which is to say the parts that counted most for the KMT – while leaving the subsistence economy of the countryside where the CCP lived relatively intact.

The Communists, having been delivered from destruction by Japanese aggression in 1936, eventually arrived at a superior strategy, less patient and consistent, and more aggressively opportunistic, than is commonly supposed, but nevertheless distinguished by an appreciation for the mutual dependency of military and political action. For Chiang, military victory was a precondition for social reform. For Mao, the two went hand in hand. Yet superior strategy does not guarantee success in war. Until close to the end, the KMT was the stronger side. The war was fought to a finish because it was the only way to see who would win.

Its consequences could hardly have been greater. China, the most populous nation on earth, became subject to a regime bent upon permanent revolution, whose murderous propensities would prove second to none. The Korean War, which followed the Communist victory by a few months, would almost certainly not have been fought if the Kuomintang had prevailed. The revolutionary insurgency against the French in Indo-China likewise could not have succeeded without the logistical support and physical sanctuary provided by Vietnam's long border with post-revolutionary China, a fact of which the Viet Minh leadership would make no secret, despite their own well-founded fears of their powerful neighbour. And of course, without the initial Communist success in the north, the final conflict between North and South Vietnam would never have occurred, sparing both Vietnam and the United States the worst that the Cold War had to offer. By any reckoning, the war for mastery in China was an exercise in the sowing of dragon's teeth.

CHAPTER TWO

Korea

An elderly North Korean peasant walks past a camouflaged gun along the Imjin River.

Korea

There are neither two suns in the sky, nor two kings in the country.

The Book of Rites

IN THE EARLY hours of 25 June 1950 forward artillery units of the North Korean People's Army (NKPA) opened fire on their counterparts in the army of the Republic of Korea (ROK), dug in a few miles to the south. Such incidents had been common for months. This time, however, the firing announced a general advance by seven well-equipped divisions, spearheaded by an armoured brigade mounting Soviet-supplied T-34 tanks. Seoul, 30 miles away, fell after three days. By the end of July, NKPA units pouring down the western half of the country had reached the water separating Korea and Japan.

Two months later, when American and ROK forces stood poised for their own offensive going the other way, the US ambassador to the United Nations would describe the line across which the first shots of the Korean War had been fired as 'imaginary'. It had not seemed so at the time. Any account of the war fought to erase it must begin with a discussion of how it came to be drawn.

Korea, whose history as a cultural nation extends to the Bronze Age, had long been a special object of Japanese ambition. The Treaty of Portsmouth, which ended the Russo-Japanese War in 1905 and won Theodore Roosevelt the Nobel Peace Prize, recognized the primacy of Japan's interests there. Five years later, when Japanese intrigue toppled the last Choson emperor, Tokyo was allowed to colonize the peninsula without interference. Popular resistance, already of long standing, accelerated after the First World War, whose settlement seemed to hold out the hope of justice to subject nations everywhere. In March 1919, peaceful demonstrations demanding independence brought what may have been 2 million people into the streets of Seoul. They were suppressed with much fury. Thousands were killed. Others fled. Later a government in exile was set up in Shanghai under the presidency of Syngman Rhee, an aristocrat collaterally descended from the old imperial line. A new element was added with the founding of the Korean Communist Party in 1925. In the 1930s its leadership passed into the hands of Kim Song-ju, who adopted the *nom de guerre* Kim Il-sung in tribute to an early martyr of the anti-Japanese resistance.

When Japanese forces moved into Manchuria in 1931 Korea was placed under military rule. A diffuse guerrilla war ensued in which Kim played a much mythologized role. To this day the partisan war against the Japanese is an important legitimizing prop for the North Korean regime. Militarily, however, the movement was of no consequence. Korea saw no serious fighting during the Second World War. Its partition was a political rather than a military event, arising from Allied plans to disarm the Japanese forces stuck there when the war ended.

The Korean question was first broached among the Allies at the Cairo Conference in 1943, where a pledge was extracted from Stalin that the country would receive independence 'in due course'. Later on it was decided that Soviet forces, due to enter the war against Japan in August 1945, would occupy Korea above the 38th Parallel – a line without significance in Korean history, chosen to facilitate the repatriation of Japanese troops by placing the ports of Inchon and Pusan at the disposal of the United States Navy. At that time the nearest American forces, who were supposed to take charge in the south, were 600 miles away on Okinawa. When they finally reached Inchon in September a puppet regime with Kim at its head was already established at Seoul. It withdrew to Pyongyang, whereupon barriers and checkpoints manned by Soviet and Northern troops grew up along the 38th Parallel. A scheme to establish an inter-Allied trusteeship for the entire country was rejected by all Korean nationalists except the communists, who laid exclusive claim, with Stalin's backing, to deal with the Allies on Korea's behalf. The US baulked, and appealed to the United Nations. Supervised national elections were called for, but the Soviets refused to co-operate, and in the event they were held only in the South. Syngman Rhee, brought back from exile under American protection, was chosen President. His government was set up in Seoul in August 1948. Kim's regime declared itself the People's Republic of Korea a few weeks later.

Military preparations proceeded against this background, more vigorously in the North, which by 1950 possessed 135,000 regular soldiers, equipped and trained by Soviet advisers. Forces in the South were comparably large, but were organized as a constabulary force, without heavy weapons. Half were engaged against guerrillas sponsored by the North, 30,000 of whom were killed by the South Korean Army and police. The remaining ROK forces manned the intra-Korean border, a scene of raids and bombardments by both sides beginning in May 1949. Later on the United States would be criticized for having failed to provide South Korea with heavy arms like those the Soviets supplied to the North. It did not do so largely because it did not

A forest of residential chimneys outside Seoul bears witness to the destructiveness of the initial Northern attack. After the war such scenes would be common on both sides of the 38th Parallel.

wish to provoke a confrontation in a region where its ultimate attitude was still uncertain in the minds of policy-makers. It also suspected that Rhee's government, no less than Kim's, would not hesitate to seek reunification by force of arms, if it had them.

It is difficult to imagine any formula for Korean independence that would not have given rise to some kind of civil war. The long Japanese occupation had created its share of winners (a few) and losers (many), and once it ended, a bloody reckoning was unavoidable. What such a war might have looked like can probably be guessed from the insurgency conducted against the South in 1948–9, and perhaps also from the periodic acts of slaughter visited upon civilians by both Korean armies as they passed back and forth across the peninsula in the first year of the war. In any event, there is no question that the successful suppression of guerrilla insurgency in the South is among the factors that explains the timing of the Northern attack. Another is the return to the North of large numbers of battle-hardened Korean troops, who had served with the Chinese Communists in Manchuria.

American and Soviet forces, less a few hundred Soviet advisers, were gone from Korea by the end of 1949. Kim did not expect them to return. Early in 1950 he went to Moscow to confirm Stalin's support for a move against the South, and was told that Soviet forces would not intervene to help him; though Stalin did order that Kim's requests for arms and *matériel* be met, as they would be throughout the war. Whether Stalin thought the United States would fight in Korea is a matter of conjecture. He was obviously not indifferent to the nature of the regime established there: when Kim Il-sung returned to Korea, after all, he was wearing the uniform of a captain in the Red Army. Yet Stalin's main concern was the rapidly concretizing stand-off in Europe, and he may simply have regarded any conflict in Asia as a useful diversion of American effort from that more critical region. He certainly intended that events unfolding in Korea should hold limited liability for the Soviet Union.

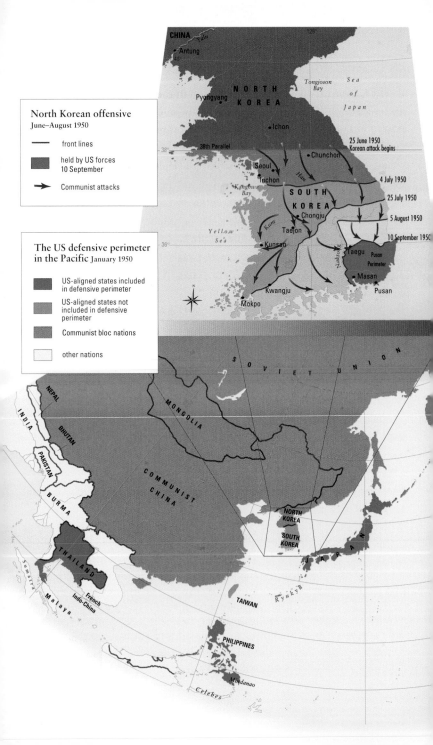

North Korean offensive
June–August 1950

— front lines

held by US forces
10 September

→ Communist attacks

The US defensive perimeter
in the Pacific January 1950

US-aligned states included
in defensive perimeter

US-aligned states not
included in defensive
perimeter

Communist bloc nations

other nations

CHINA

Palu

• Antung

NORTH
KOREA

Pyongyang •

Tongjoson
Bay

Sea
of
Japan

• Ichon

38th Parallel

38°

25 June 1950
Korean attack begins

Seoul •

• Chunchon

Inchon •

Han

Kanghwa
Bay

SOUTH
KOREA

• Chongju

4 July 1950

25 July 1950

Kum

Taejon

5 August 1950

10 September 1950

Yellow
Sea

36°

• Kunsan

Naktong

Taegu

Pusan
Perimeter

• Masan

• Kwangju

Pusan

• Mokpo

SOVIET   UNION

NEPAL

INDIA

BHUTAN

MONGOLIA

PAKISTAN

BURMA

COMMUNIST
CHINA

THAILAND

French
Indo-China

NORTH
KOREA

SOUTH
KOREA

J   A   P   A   N

Sumatra

Malaya

TAIWAN

Ryukyu

PHILIPPINES

Mindanao

Celebes

The US for its part had achieved much in the way of obscuring its intentions, even from itself. At the ceremony proclaiming South Korea's existence, Douglas MacArthur, Supreme Commander of US forces in the Pacific, put his hand on Syngman Rhee's shoulder and told him he would defend Korea as if it were California. Thereafter, however, Rhee was repeatedly cautioned that American assistance would only follow an unprovoked attack, a formulation that was obviously intended as much to restrain as to reassure. Officially, the United States had declared that its fundamental interests in Asia lay along the off-shore island chains descending south from Japan through the Ryukyus to the Philippines and Taiwan; to which explanations were occasionally added to the

NORTH KOREAN OFFENSIVE, JUNE–AUGUST 1950

Like most modern conventional wars, the Korean War began with an overwhelming offensive intended to achieve a rapid decision quickly. Failure in such cases is also usually decisive. Once American forces reached Korea in large numbers, the expulsion of Northern forces from the South was assured.

effect that such statements were not intended to rule anyone or anything out. In May 1950, the Chairman of the Senate Foreign Relations Committee said that he thought the communists would probably overrun Korea 'whether we want it or not'. A month later he was almost proved right.

Under the circumstances, the rapid return of American forces to the Korean peninsula amounted to something like strategic surprise, always a rare thing in war, and in this case decisive. Thrown in piecemeal and poorly equipped, US troops pouring in from Japan fared badly at first. By the end of July, however, US and ROK forces already outnumbered their opponents, whose energy and cohesion had begun to flag as a consequence of their headlong advance. In early August, a stable defensive line was finally held north and west of Pusan, against which NKPA forces beat in vain.

A breakout was only a matter of time. It came in mid September, following an amphibious assault against the port of Inchon, deep in the enemy rear. The operation was a feat of arms, pushed forward by MacArthur over the apprehensions of his own subordinates, and carried out in the face of formidable physical difficulties, above all the treacherous tides of Inchon itself, which rise and fall by 30 feet in a day. Although resistance in the landing zone was light, it stiffened as American forces pressed inland towards Seoul. By the time the city fell, on 27 September, the entire NKPA position in the South had disintegrated.

The toll exacted by the Northern attack had been terrible. Southern casualties, civilian and military, totalled a quarter of a million. Half were fatal. Almost 600,000 houses had been damaged or destroyed. American

AMERICAN COUNTER-OFFENSIVE, SEPTEMBER–OCTOBER 1950
The UN counter-offensive that began with the amphibious assault at Inchon rapidly drove the North Korean army from the South. The decision to exploit this success by pressing north above the 38th Parallel would transform the war into a direct struggle with the Chinese, whose forces were already poised to intervene.

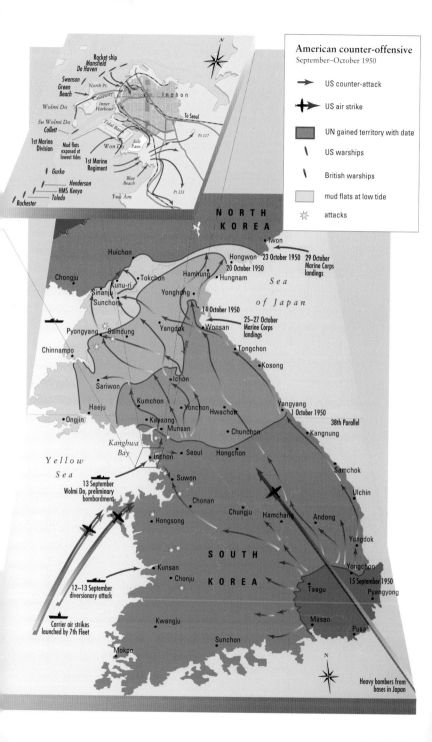

American counter-offensive
September–October 1950

→ US counter-attack

⟶✈⟵ US air strike

■ UN gained territory with date

\ US warships

\ British warships

mud flats at low tide

✳ attacks

Rocket ship
Mansfield
De Haven
Swenson
Green Beach
North Pt.
Inchon
Wolmi Do
Inner Harbour
To Seoul
Su Wolmi Do
Tidal Basin
Collett
Pt 117
1st Marine Division
Mud flats exposed at lowest tides
Won Do
Salt Pans
Gurke
1st Marine Regiment
Henderson
HMS Kenya
Toledo
Blue Beach
Rochester
Tok Am
Pt 233

NORTH KOREA

Iwon
Huichon
Hongwon   23 October 1950   29 October Marine Corps landings
20 October 1950
Chongju
Tokchon   Hamhung
Kunu-ri   Hamhung   Hungnam
Sinanju   Yonghung   Sea
Suchon
14 October 1950   of Japan
Pyongyang   Yangdok   Wonsan   25–27 October Marine Corps landings
Samdung
Chinnampo   Tongchon
Kosong
Ichon
Sariwon
Kumchon   Yonchon   Hwachon
Haeju   Yangyang   1 October 1950
Kaesong   38th Parallel
Ongjin   Munsan   Chunchon   Kangnung
Kanghwa Bay   Hongchon
Yellow   Inchon   Seoul   Hongchon
Sea   Suwon   Samchok
13 September   Chonan   Ulchin
Wolmi Do, preliminary bombardment
Chungju   Hamchang   Andong
Hongsong   Yongdok
SOUTH   Yongchon
Kunsan   KOREA   15 September 1950
Chonju   Taegu   Pyangyong
12–13 September diversionary attack   Masan   Pusan
Carrier air strikes   Kwangju
launched by 7th Fleet   Sunchon
Mokpo   N
Heavy bombers from bases in Japan

dead approached 3,000, with another 15,000 wounded or missing. It was now necessary to decide what to do about it. Since the end of June, US and ROK forces, gradually joined by units from a dozen other nations, had acted under a UN resolution calling upon all members to repel the North's aggression. In the United States the resolution effectively substituted for a constitutionally required declaration of war. This would become a source of much condescension among opponents of the Truman administration, to whom the approved expression 'police action' became synonymous with pusillanimity. Yet it is a fact that, since the founding of the United Nations, a legal state of war – an expression sufficiently paradoxical in itself – cannot exist for its members. Had the Korean War ended with the repulse of the North in September, however, such niceties would have mattered to no one. Their place in America's pantheon of bitter ironies derives from the decision to pursue NKPA forces beyond the 38th Parallel in October, in order to create a unified, non-communist Korean state.

US forces coming ashore at Inchon, 15 September 1950. US Marines suffered about 200 casualties securing their beachhead, including twenty killed, far fewer than might have been anticipated, given America's experiences against the Japanese in the Pacific.

Discussion of such a contingency had begun in Washington in mid July, which is to say a week or so after the subject came up in Beijing. Mao never imagined that American intervention could have any object other than the destruction of North Korea. Like Stalin, he had personally backed Kim's plans against the South, a fact of which Kim had made good use in his dealings with the Soviets, already wary of China's influence in Asia. These apprehensions were not misplaced. Among Mao's motives for entering the Korean War, a desire to reassert China's historical role as the supreme arbiter of Asian affairs was probably the most important. The defeat of the North would also threaten Manchuria, the vital base from which the Chinese revolution had been won. By the time UN forces began moving into the North, Chinese troops were already organizing to meet them.

This was a possibility MacArthur's headquarters had discounted, despite ample diplomatic warning. His complacency rested on three mutually reinforcing miscalculations: first, that a swift encirclement of surviving NKPA forces would be achieved well below the Chinese frontier, thanks to a second amphibious operation against the Northern coast at Wonson; second, that Chinese forces venturing below the Yalu River would be broken by superior firepower; and finally, that American nuclear weapons would deter China from

intervening in Korea no matter what. As it turned out, however, the envelopment failed to close as intended, partly from administrative breakdown and exhaustion among the units tasked to carry out the main assault; partly because landing operations at Wonson were held up by North Korean mines. The hoped-for encirclement thus turned into straightforward pursuit, spearheaded by ROK units whose approach to the Yalu River line was supposed to be less provocative than that of their American allies.

On 25 October an ROK division moving north at Unsan made contact with what proved to be the forward elements of a Chinese army of almost 200,000 men. Within a few weeks UN forces were in retreat everywhere, sometimes in disarray, sometimes resisting tenaciously, as at the Chosin Reservoir, where the 1st Marine Division fought a fierce action to escape encirclement in early December. It was not until mid January that the momentum of the Chinese offensive was spent, by which time the fighting front had been pushed well into the South.

The biggest battles of the Korean War were fought in the winter and spring of 1951, when UN forces blunted the final communist offensives and fought their way back north of Seoul. By then doubts had arisen within the Truman administration and the Joint Chiefs of Staff as to whether the campaign to roll back communism in North Korea could be resumed at an acceptable cost in lives. There were also larger strategic risks to consider. Like their Soviet counterparts, American policy-makers were dogged by concern for the military balance in Europe, still burdened by problems of post-war reconstruction, with a disarmed and divided Germany at its centre. Within this alarming vacuum the new NATO alliance could deploy little more than a theory – nuclear deterrence – plus conventional forces far smaller than those of its prospective adversary. At bottom, the problem was an old one. It had arisen at the outset of the Second World War, when it became necessary to decide which of two great theatres, Europe or Asia, would be the main focus of Allied effort. The answer then had been 'Europe First', and that was the answer now. The limit had been reached.

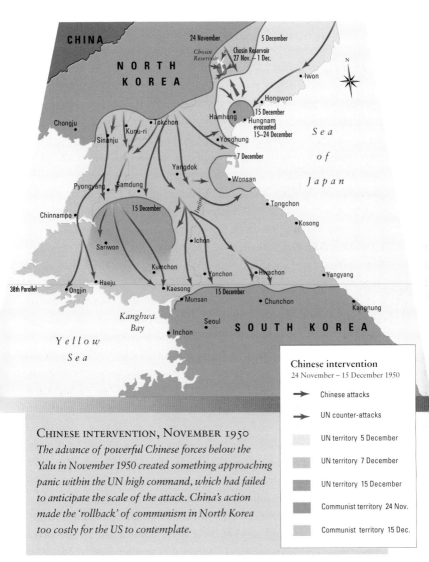

CHINA

24 November   5 December

Chosin Reservoir   Chosin Reservoir
                     27 Nov. – 1 Dec.

N O R T H
K O R E A

• Iwon

N

• Hongwon

15 December

Chongju   • Tokchon   Hamhung   Hungnam
                              • evacuated
Kunu-ri   15–24 December   *S e a*
Sinanju   • Yonghung

7 December   *o f*

Yangdok
•   • Wonsan   *J a p a n*

Pyongyang   Samdung   • Tongchon

Chinnampo •   15 December   Imjin

Sariwon   • Ichon   • Kosong

Kumchon
• Yonchon • Hwachon   • Yangyang

38th Parallel • Ongjin • Haeju • Kaesong   15 December

• Munsan   • Chunchon   Kangnung

Kanghwa   Seoul   S O U T H   K O R E A
Bay   • Inchon

Y e l l o w

S e a

Chinese intervention
24 November – 15 December 1950

→   Chinese attacks

→   UN counter-attacks

     UN territory 5 December

     UN territory 7 December

     UN territory 15 December

     Communist territory 24 Nov.

     Communist territory 15 Dec.

CHINESE INTERVENTION, NOVEMBER 1950
The advance of powerful Chinese forces below the
Yalu in November 1950 created something approaching
panic within the UN high command, which had failed
to anticipate the scale of the attack. China's action
made the 'rollback' of communism in North Korea
too costly for the US to contemplate.

Douglas MacArthur disagreed, as well he might, having fought his
part of the Second World War at the far end of a logistical food chain
tailored to the needs of a conflict on the other side of the world.
MacArthur had always believed that Asia was as important as Europe.
He also thought the moral stakes in Korea were sufficiently compelling

to justify any level of military effort, up to nuclear war; and that success in Korea would provide a basis for reversing the results of the Chinese revolution. These views were no secret to his superiors, but in April 1951 he wrote them down in a letter to the Minority Leader of the House of Representatives, Joseph Martin, who published the letter. MacArthur was duly sacked for insubordination, but also because since Inchon he had become disturbingly erratic, veering between bold promises of rapid success and dire predictions of impending disaster when the successes failed to materialize. He was unwilling to tolerate any sort of compromise, a fact that Harry Truman would later claim had weighed heavily in his decision. Hardly anyone would have thought MacArthur was the right man to wage the war that now needed to be waged, the sole purpose of which was to force a negotiated settlement.

Ground operations during the last two years of the Korean War were confined to a fortified line anchored at both ends by the sea. Its static nature, the dominant role of heavy weapons and the elaborate entrenchments used by both sides have inspired comparisons with the Western Front in the First World War. The resemblance is superficial. In France after 1914 one sees a strategic stalemate created by tactical facts, which gave overwhelming advantages to whoever stood on the defensive. In Korea, one sees a tactical stalemate created by strategic facts, specifically the disinclination of either side to risk escalation or heavy losses in return for gains that might simply be bargained away.

Even in the war's early, mobile phase, UN operations had been subject to detailed political review, hammered out in discussions between the United States, the ROK and their European allies. Once negotiations to end the war began, ground combat was linked to the vicissitudes of the truce talks. Military actions became rhetorical exercises, intended to convey resolve, punctuate a demand, reward a concession, and so on. Communist attacks, for instance, were usually concentrated against ROK forces, but might shift against US-held positions if the moment seemed right to remind American opinion of the costs incurred by refusing to settle. The UN, on the other hand,

A 155mm howitzer shell explodes in the distance, illuminating the gun that fired it. By October 1952, when this picture was taken, the Korean War had evolved into a contest of raids and bombardments, with no prospect of serious advance by either side.

preferred to conduct the war of messages from the air, which rendered the signal-to-noise ratio of its ground operations even lower than it might otherwise have been. The most promising approach called for a slow but steady push northwards, aiming at the peninsula's 'narrow waist' above Wonson, where the shortest and strongest defensive line could be created. Although such gradual pressure seemed consonant with the requirements of the bargaining table, the negative impact on Western opinion of additional casualties, plus the likelihood that the talks would break down if the Northern capital were threatened, ruled it out. Most UN attacks sought local tactical advantages. It is not for nothing that so many battles in the last two years of the Korean War are named after hills.

The onset of negotiations lent additional significance to UN air operations. From the first days of the war, American air superiority had been vital in slowing the NKPA's advance, and buying time for the build-up around Pusan. American planes also tried to interdict

A strafing attack by elements of the 5th US Air Force, photographed by a photo-reconnaissance plane that accompanied them. US tactical air power was vital in halting both major communist offensives. About half of all North Korean and Chinese tanks destroyed in the South were attacked from the air.

Chinese forces moving south by attacking the bridges across the Yalu River. These operations met serious resistance from Chinese and Soviet air forces, whose bases north of the river were immune from direct assault. As the war dragged on, tactical strikes against troop concentrations and military communications were supplemented by a strategic bombing campaign of considerable proportions. Napalm, a new invention, was much employed as an improvement on the incendiary bombs used to set fire to Japanese cities in the Second World War. The most intense period came in the summer of 1952 – the low point of diplomatic stalemate – during which 90 per cent of North Korea's electrical generating capacity was destroyed, and vast areas were flooded following air attacks on Northern dams. On 29 August 1,400 planes bombed Pyongyang, the single largest raid of the war.

As always in the conduct of strategic bombing, some uncertainty prevailed as to the nature of the target being struck. Although the physical effects of the air campaign were incontestably horrendous, its psychological impact remained elusive. The most pronounced results in this area may have been achieved by a weapon that was never used: the atomic bomb. Its presence in the American arsenal was never far from the minds of Chinese and North Korean decision-makers. US army doctrine in 1950 did not distinguish between atomic and conventional weapons. The former were regarded as a legitimate resource of battlefield commanders, and plans to employ them in a variety of contexts were developed throughout the war. Practice bombing runs were even carried out, in which solitary B-29s were dispatched from Okinawa to drop dummy weapons against targets in the North, an unnerving spectacle in itself.

Nevertheless, there was no question that the actual discharge of nuclear weapons was a political act, and constraints at that level were formidable. President Truman first mentioned the possibility that atomic weapons might be necessary to stem the Chinese onslaught at a news conference in November 1950, and immediately found himself face to face with the British Prime Minister, Clement Attlee, who had flown to Washington to remonstrate with his alliance partner. Dwight Eisenhower, Truman's successor, was likewise restrained by Attlee's successor, Winston Churchill. Eisenhower's military reputation is widely thought to have contributed in some general way to the conclusion of an armistice in 1953. Yet he never spoke publicly about using nuclear weapons in Korea. Nor did he authorize the deployment of atomic warheads in the western Pacific, as Truman did. Churchill, in any case, left his old comrade in no doubt that escalation in Korea would mean the end of the European alliance, if not the annihilation of Europe. Given that the most plausible targets for nuclear strikes were in Manchuria, it was also necessary to consider that Soviet air forces deployed there included bombers capable of retaliating against the air bases launching the attacks, in Japan – a possibility that seemed to short-circuit the still imperfectly understood logic of global deterrence.

Talks to end the fighting in Korea began in July 1951, following a month of peace feelers by all major parties to the conflict. This suggested just the sort of mutual exhaustion that should have been conducive to a settlement. The UN negotiators envisioned a two-step process, with military questions addressed first and political issues deferred until fighting had ceased. Trouble arose about where exactly the ceasefire line should be, and talks were suspended for a while because of provocative actions by both sides. When the talks resumed, however, general terms for disengagement emerged relatively smoothly. By December the basic dimensions of a truce on the ground were in place, and attention shifted to arrangements for administering them. It was on one of these issues that the proceedings broke down.

International law respecting prisoners of war is designed to ensure that prisoners are treated humanely, and allowed to go home when hostilities end. At the time of the Korean War there were no recognized rules governing the treatment of prisoners who did not want to go home; though there was already reason to wish there were. After the Second World War, thousands of Soviet POWs liberated by Western armies were forcibly repatriated to the Soviet Union despite their most fervent pleas for sanctuary. Some committed suicide rather than return. Most of the rest were jailed or executed upon arrival, on suspicion of having collaborated with the Germans. This bitter experience cast its shadow over Korea, where UN negotiators proposed that the principle of voluntary repatriation be observed by both sides. The communists refused, for reasons that became obvious after a Red Cross canvass in April 1952 revealed that fewer than half of North Korean and Chinese prisoners would willingly be sent back.

Given that the North had always claimed to be fighting a people's war, to which Chinese volunteers had lent comradely support, a more grievous ideological humiliation was difficult to imagine. Charges of fraud, coercion and brainwashing followed. Threats were made to try captured American pilots as war criminals. Prison populations in the

A North Korean prisoner eating 'C' rations. Behind him lie the bodies of two US Marines. Disputes over the rights of Communist POWs became a central issue in the negotiations to end the Korean War, which was prolonged by many months as a consequence.

South were infiltrated and mobilized to resist camp authorities. In one famous incident, the American commandant on Koje Island was taken prisoner, and forced to accede to demands for more humane conditions, an episode embarrassing to UN negotiators, who would obviously have liked to have the POW issue all to themselves.

Productive talks did not resume until 1953. In February, UN negotiators put forward a Red Cross proposal that sick and wounded prisoners who wished to return should be exchanged as a gesture of goodwill. At the end of March it was, surprisingly, accepted. Explanations as to why vary, but never omit the fact that, on 5 March, Joseph Stalin died after a brief illness. His unexpected passing created a succession crisis in the Soviet Union, and an opportunity for a general reappraisal of Soviet strategy, which until this point had failed to achieve what had always been its primary objective: to divide the United States from its European allies. On the contrary: over the course of the Korean War conditions in Eastern Europe had deteriorated, while NATO had survived its birth throes sufficiently to begin contemplating the admission of a rearmed Germany to its ranks. American military spending had tripled, conscription had been reintroduced, and anti-communism had become the lingua franca of American politics. A less confrontational policy could not have done worse, and would now be tried.

What Stalin's death may have meant to Mao can only be guessed. Perhaps it was simply an opportunity to draw a line under a policy that had served its purpose – to demonstrate Chinese strength and independence – but which otherwise had no natural terminus. Kim's regime in the North, the symbol and object of China's sacrifices, was now certain to survive. This being so, signals from the new Eisenhower administration that it would not tolerate stalemate much longer – including support for dramatic expansion of ROK force structure, and a declaration that the US Seventh Fleet would not restrain the Chinese Nationalists on Taiwan – may have made some impression, though no public sign was given. Everyone knew, however, that Eisenhower had gained his office partly on the strength of a promise to reduce defence spending. That promise could not be kept unless something changed in Korea, one way or another.

The exchange of sick and wounded prisoners, Operation Little Switch, occurred at the end of April. By then, planning for Big Switch was well under way. The voluntary principle would apply: anyone wishing to return home would be sent back. Those who did not would be turned over to a neutral international commission, and interviewed by representatives of their own armies. If they still refused repatriation, they would be allowed to go where they wished. Before the final exchange could be implemented, however, Syngman Rhee, in defiance of his American sponsors, ordered that North Korean prisoners desiring to remain in the South should simply be released *en masse*. Rhee had never accepted the idea that fighting should cease before Korea was unified. And while his astonishing gesture proved insufficient to derail the armistice, finally concluded (without his signature) on 27 July, it was a reminder of who the original contestants in the Korean War had been.

The Korean War is remembered as a paradigmatic example of limited war, in which military actions at every level are hemmed in by complex political requirements. It is a reasonable description unless you are Korean, as many as 3 million of whom may have been killed (10 per cent of the total population). In relative terms, Europe suffered no worse in the Second World War. China got more or less what it bargained for. It demonstrated that its revolution could not be reversed by force, and that it had what it took to face down a nuclear foe. Although it is easy to assume that the price was higher than Mao had intended, even that is conjectural. Chinese casualties numbered in the high hundreds of thousands, a terrible toll that is nevertheless dwarfed by the millions who perished inside China during the years when the new regime was establishing itself. The Korean War is remembered as a victory in China, and nowhere else on earth.

Other than Korea, the big loser was the Soviet Union, which would henceforth be obliged to regard China as something like an equal within the communist world. Stalin did his successors no favour by alerting Americans to the military requirements of containment, a policy that had initially been conceived mainly in economic and political terms. It was in Korea that the United States demonstrated – one might even say discovered – that it was prepared to resist communist expansion by force, even in regions not previously thought vital to its interests. When the war ended it had bound itself to defend South Korea in perpetuity, a result barely imaginable when US troops first set foot there in 1945. Asia, if not quite first, would no longer be second.

CHAPTER THREE

Southeast Asia

*Chinese members of the Malayan Home
Guard learn how to assemble a carbine.
The British willingness to arm and train
Malayan Chinese to carry out local security
tasks did much to establish their credibility
with the squatter populations on whom the
rebels depended.*

Southeast Asia

The white man is finished in Asia.

Ho Chi Minh (1945)

IN JUNE 1940, the French philosopher Simone Weil took note of the appearance of German soldiers in the streets of Paris by commenting in her diary that it was a great day for the people of Indo-China. Her remark set a standard for emotional detachment that has rarely been matched by subsequent observers of post-colonial conflict in Southeast Asia. When Weil made her lapidary observation, all the countries in the region except Thailand were controlled by Western powers: Indonesia by the Dutch; Indo-China (Vietnam, Laos and Cambodia) by France; the Philippines by the United States; Burma, Malaya and Singapore by Great Britain. With the exception of the United States, which took possession of the Philippines following its victory over Spain in 1898, all these powers had been drawn to the region by its natural and agricultural resources, and because of its strategic location between India and China, athwart the sea lanes connecting Europe and East Asia.

As European power and prestige declined with the onset of war in 1939, these attractions grew in the eyes of Japan, ultimately tempting it into a final, fatal expansion of the war it had begun in China in 1937. From 1942 to 1945 Southeast Asia became part of the Greater East Asian Co-Prosperity Sphere, a thinly veiled effort to substitute one imperial structure for another. Japanese expansionism hastened the maturation of nationalist movements that already existed before the war. Some became anti-Japanese as well as anti-Western, others did not. They also diverged in their social orientation.

Colonial economies in Southeast Asia were organized to produce agricultural goods and raw materials for international consumption. This modernizing process had diverse social effects. As in Europe a century earlier, the emergence of a commoditized, market-oriented economy undermined traditional agriculture and drove smallholders off the land, either from indebtedness or in search of jobs that paid a cash wage. Others prospered by accumulating the land thus freed up, or by adapting themselves to new opportunities that participation in world trade created. Neither group necessarily relished being ruled by foreigners, though the latter were more willing to collaborate with the Japanese, particularly early in the war. In the broadest terms, those who had succeeded within the colonial economy tended to see the national cause as a matter of seizing the productive apparatus the West had created. Those who sought to base themselves upon the pauperized peasantry and (still miniscule) urban proletariat were inclined to see nationalism as a framework for radical social reform. Once the Japanese had gone, these differences became the basic structural divide around which national conflicts would organize themselves.

The construction of nation states in Southeast Asia was a violent process everywhere, but with marked differences in scale and consequences. Thailand was the best situated. Never colonized by the West, it was an independent ally of Japan during the war, which provided an occasion to annex territory from neighbouring Cambodia, Laos and Malaya. Afterwards it had to return these lands, but beyond that its post-war tribulations were confined to recurring *coups d'état*, which cut short an initial experiment in republicanism and produced a series of pro-American military governments. The American bombing campaign against North Vietnam would be based partly in Thailand, testimony, if nothing else, to Bangkok's perennial confidence that it can hold its own in a rough neighbourhood.

The native leadership in Burma was also well-disposed towards Japan, which recognized an independent (military) government in Rangoon in 1943. As the war shifted against the Japanese, however, their Burmese clients did too, and turned to partisan warfare in co-operation with the British at the end of 1944. Although Britain sought to retain its links to Burma by offering it dominion status after the war, popular protests rendered Burma ungovernable on this basis. The government, based upon the army, declared itself independent outside the Commonwealth in 1948.

Ever since, Burma has been beset by recurring guerrilla wars by ethnic minorities, often concentrated in geographically remote areas, that had first been mobilized against the Japanese, and then excluded from the post-war settlement. Burma's case is thus a reminder that, in terms of its human geography, most of Southeast Asia is no better suited than the Balkans to the smooth working out of 'national self-determination'. Although Burma's recurring insurgencies have often been infiltrated or even dominated by communists, their roots lie in the subterranean ethnic exclusivity that is so often characteristic of authoritarian regimes. These uprisings have not seriously threatened to seize power in Burma since the early 1950s, when fighting was occasionally severe. Yet they remain, after fifty years, an obstacle to the demilitarization of the Burmese state.

Somewhat similar conditions arose in Indonesia. Indonesia was the only Western colony in Southeast Asia that did not produce meaningful anti-Japanese resistance. This is a tribute to the exploitative character of Dutch rule, under which the country had fallen in the seventeenth century. Long-simmering resentment acquired organized form in 1912 with the formation of the Islamic Association, a cultural movement that allowed grievances against the Dutch to be fitted into a framework that transcended local interests. A sharper edge was added with the founding of the Indonesian Communist Party (PKI) in 1924, and the Indonesian Nationalist Party (PNI) in 1927.

Although the PKI was driven underground within a few years, the PNI survived as a (barely audible) voice of public opposition. Its leadership proved adept at collaborating with the Japanese, who needed well-educated and experienced people to replace the Dutch colonial administration. These the PNI supplied, in exchange for political concessions and military training for the Indonesian Army. Although the Japanese gradually conceived doubts as to the loyalty of their clients, there was little they could do about it as the war continued

Achmed Sukarno in 1949. Sukarno was the central figure in Indonesia's independence movement. Later, as the country's first president (1949–66), he suppressed parliamentary government in favour of 'Guided Democracy,' a euphemism for authoritarian rule.

to drag on. At the end of 1944 Japan declared its intention to grant Indonesia full sovereignty, a belated attempt to make good on its earlier pronouncements about 'Asia for Asians'. In the event, the defeat of the Japanese became the signal for Indonesian independence, proclaimed by PNI chairman Achmed Sukarno three days after Tokyo's surrender was announced.

Sukarno's declaration did not go uncontested. The Dutch assumed their rights would be respected after the war, an outlook backed up by British and Dutch troops dispatched to receive the surrender of Japanese forces and attend to the repatriation of POWs. From the British perspective, the restoration of Dutch authority was synonymous with the maintenance of order. The result was disorder, amounting at times to pitched battle, notably at Surabaya in October–November

1945, which held out for three weeks against superior British forces. Twenty-two British soldiers and twenty-eight officers, including one general, were killed. Thereafter Britain's policy shifted towards mediation. The Dutch remained adamant. In their eyes, Indonesian nationalism was, in effect, Javanese imperialism, Java being the most populous and economically developed island of an archipelago whose historical unity was, in fact, a product of the Dutch presence. They proposed to create a federal regime in which individual islands and island groups sharing common ethnicity would receive autonomy under Dutch oversight. Agreement to this effect was reached at the end of 1946, but broke down at once. Two more rounds of serious fighting followed, culminating in the capture of most of the republican leadership in December 1948.

By then, however, military success had been rendered moot by a rising tide of international criticism. In January 1949, a conference of nineteen Asian nations at New Delhi called upon the UN to recognize Indonesian sovereignty. The United States threatened to cut off Marshall Plan aid to the Netherlands unless serious negotiations were begun. The Dutch conceded in May. In all, as many as 100,000 Indonesians may have died in their war of liberation, along with 2,500 Dutch soldiers. Later on, Dutch claims about the imperfections of Indonesian nationalism would be vindicated, as the new state confronted secessionist movements in Kalimantan, the Celebes, the Moloccas, Irian Jaya, and East Timor, a former Portuguese colony annexed by Indonesia in 1976.

If resistance to the Japanese was weakest in Indonesia, it was most tenacious in the Philippines. Once the war ended, however, national reconstruction proceeded apace, pursuant to American promises of independence dating back to the 1930s. By 1946 a new regime was in place, based upon large landowners and businessmen who had prospered under the Americans. It immediately faced the familiar problem of disarming wartime allies whose share of post-war power was not what had been hoped for. Among these the fiercest were the

Hukbalahap, whose name is a Tagálog acronym meaning 'People's Anti-Japanese Army'. The Huks were the military arm of the Philippine Communist Party, with a strong base among the impoverished peasantry in the rice-growing regions of Luzon. Although a number of Communists, including the Huk leader Luis Taruc, won seats in the first post-war parliamentary election, they were excluded from government on the grounds that they represented a terrorist organization. The Huks then reverted to their jungle hideaways, seized a number of large estates and set up their own regime in central Luzon. The new government in Manila pledged to crush the Huks in a self-described 'mailed fist' campaign, which amounted to little more than indiscriminate intimidation, aimed at the rural population. Its alienation deepened, while the government's prestige fell dangerously low.

It was not until 1950 that an effective response was developed, under the leadership of a new Minister of Defence, Raymon Magsaysay. Magsaysay, with the help of an American counter-insurgency expert, Edward Lansdale, devised a campaign that combined ruthlessness and conciliation. Magsaysay curtailed the random brutality of the Philippine Army, while rewarding its more purposeful forms: under his administration, killing Huks became the only route to promotion. Habeas corpus and other limitations on the right to interrogate suspects were suspended, a politically risky decision that paid off by allowing the development of reliable intelligence about the structure of the Huk organization. As a consequence, much of the Huk leadership was captured on the eve of a planned move against Manila itself.

The spectre of betrayal thereafter haunted the Huks, whose conduct became more randomly terroristic. This increased the willingness of the population to inform on them. At the same time, Magsaysay undertook a large-scale programme to clear new land on Luzon, by which the land hunger that fuelled the revolt was assuaged. Food and medical aid were also supplied, distributed by the same troops conducting the counter-insurgency effort. Huks who turned themselves in were given amnesty, plus a share of the new land. American money funded this effort, just as it paid to rearm the Philippine Army, whose lack of firepower had been part of the reason for its initial failure to engage the Huks effectively. Yet the American role was not particularly visible to Filipinos, which contributed to the campaign's success. In 1953, Magsaysay was elected President of the Philippines. His nemesis, Taruc, surrendered the following year.

A similarly astute combination of military and political measures were employed in the counter-insurgency campaign waged by the British in Malaya. There too the immediate cause of conflict lay in the exclusion of communist guerrillas from a share in political power. In Malaya, however, demographic conditions created by the colonial economy exerted a critical influence. In political terms British rule, which was fully established towards the end of the nineteenth century, was lightly applied, directly so only in a few coastal areas bordering the Strait of Malacca, whose control was the main point of the exercise. The country as a whole was organized as a federation of local sultanates, each with a British resident, under the supervision of a high commissioner in Kuala Lumpur.

Economically, however, Malaya was transformed by colonization. Before the arrival of the British, Malaya had been an agricultural country, 80 per cent of whose territory was undeveloped jungle. The colonizers sought to exploit its natural reserves of rubber and tin, for which they obtained the requisite labour by encouraging Chinese immigration. These immigrants provided the social base for the Malayan Communist Party (MCP), organized after 1930 as an extension of the communist movement in China itself. They suffered terribly under the Japanese, whose policy was superficially favourable to Malayan nationalism, and vigorously anti-Chinese. Trade in rubber and tin was destroyed and the immigrant labourers were forced to squat on untended land along the edges of the jungle.

The MCP, driven underground, emerged after the war in the guise of the Malayan People's Anti-Japanese Army. Numbering perhaps 7,000,

Britain, hard-pressed by international commitments around the world after 1945, drew soldiers from throughout the empire to fight in Malaya. Shown here, at their embarkation parade, are a battalion of the King's African Rifles, a mixed African and European formation comprised of volunteers from Kenya and Rhodesia.

and without heavy weapons, it had spent much of its time working on political indoctrination within the squatter communities, rather than engaging the Japanese. Nevertheless, Malaya's Chinese communists were the only military resistance movement produced during the war – their leader was accorded a place in the Victory Parade in London – which gave them a certain claim on British sympathy. An initial British proposal to reorganize Malaya in a way that would have guaranteed equal rights for the Chinese was, however, greeted as an offence by all Malayan political parties; whereupon the British backed down. The Communists, incapable of seizing power directly, surrendered their weapons and returned home.

Much hardship awaited them. Socially isolated and dependent upon shattered industries, the Chinese in Malaya were left to choose between scavenging in the overcrowded cities, or continuing their marginal existence as squatters. By mid 1948 the Federation was restored, and the way prepared for national independence on the model of India. It was against this prospect that the Malayan communists rebelled, via a campaign of sabotage and terrorism aimed at tin mines and rubber plantations. Captured documents suggest that victory was anticipated within a few months, owing to the perceived weakness of a government dependent upon foreigners, and to the fragile state of the Malayan economy, still reeling from the disruption of international trade caused by the war. In the event, however, what became known as the Malayan Emergency would last twelve years.

For three of those years the initiative lay with the guerrillas, now called the Malayan Races' Liberation Army (MRLA). British and Malayan forces at the start amounted to one battalion for every 3,000 square miles of territory. Early offensive operations against known rebel areas turned up large caches of ammunition, but inflicted few casualties. As time passed, moreover, the difficulty of providing adequate local security was bound to pose a threat to the government's legitimacy.

A start towards addressing this problem was made following the arrival of General Harold Briggs as Director of Operations in 1950. Briggs concluded that the key to the insurgency was the dependency of the guerrillas upon the Chinese squatters. These constituted the rebellion's logistical and recruitment infrastructure, which Briggs attacked by means of a massive resettlement programme.

The Briggs Plan aimed to isolate enemy fighters from their families and the rest of society. It entailed the systematic construction of hundreds of new villages. Some were designed as dormitories to house wage labourers, others as free-standing agricultural communities. All were surrounded by barbed wire and patrolled by police and Home Guard. Once completed, squatters were rounded up and moved into them, along with their transportable possessions and livestock. Their old dwellings, which tended to be widely dispersed, hence impossible to secure, were then razed. Altogether half a million people were resettled in this way.

The new villages were not prisons, though curfews were imposed and movement in and out was tightly controlled. Although Briggs reduced the effort expended pursuing armed cadres, the regulation of movement created new tactical opportunities, since, despite everything, the villages were magnets for guerrillas, who became subject to ambush along the paths leading to them. Briggs also allowed collective preventive detention, whereby not just individuals but whole communities could be confined indefinitely if any among them were suspected of supporting the guerrillas. This was the most hated measure of the war from the point of view of Malayan society. Among the guerrillas, however, that honour was reserved for the extraordinary steps taken to curtail the smuggling of food. Food stocks in the new villages were specially guarded. In some places, rice was only distributed after it had been cooked, and canned goods were opened before they were sold. In time, starvation would rate near the top among motives leading guerrillas to surrender themselves.

The Briggs Plan reshaped the social terrain on which the Malayan war would be fought, but it did not produce an immediate reversal of fortune. In October 1951, the British High Commissioner, Sir Henry Gurney, was ambushed and killed, probably the lowest point of the war on the government side. By then, civilian casualties were nearing 2,000 dead and missing, and public confidence was failing. Briggs, in poor health, retired a few months later.

Gurney's successor was General Sir Gerald Templer, who also temporarily assumed Briggs's post. Templer brought energetic personal leadership to the Malayan crisis. His first priority was to convince the population that the government would win the war. He cut back on preventive detention, and emphasized the orderly provision of police protection and regular public services. The occupants of the new villages were given ownership of the property on which they were settled, a positive attraction for many. Once areas were declared free of communists, elections were held to choose village leaders. In time, the provision of security was also made a local responsibility. Templer accelerated the expansion of native Malayan security forces begun by Briggs, and equipped them with heavier weapons and armoured vehicles, to bolster their willingness to engage the enemy, and also as a mark of confidence that they would not defect to the communists. In time, this programme extended to the creation of special units comprised of rehabilitated rebels; and also to the mobilization of primitive tribes living deep in the jungle. Finally, Templer brokered a political realignment among Malayans, by which the main nationalist party joined with its rivals representing ethnic Indians and Chinese. The resulting Alliance Party won fifty-one of fifty-two seats in the first federal election, held in 1955.

By then the communist insurgency was broken. The MCP offered to lay down its arms provided it was accepted as a legal political party. This proposal was rejected by the leader of the new assembly, Tunku Abdul Rahman, who offered individual amnesty provided the communists surrendered *en masse*. This offer too was refused. Thereafter it became general practice for government troops engaging guerrillas to call for their surrender before opening fire. Malaya achieved statehood in 1957; it was not until 1960, however, that the state of emergency, decreed in 1948, was officially lifted. In all, about 7,000 guerrillas were killed – a high percentage of their total number, which probably never exceeded 10,000. In addition, 1,346 Malayan police also died, and some 500 British and Malayan soldiers. Civilian deaths, which fell off sharply towards the end, approached 2,500.

The British campaign in Malaya has become a textbook example of successful counter-insurgency, based upon social policies designed to isolate the insurgents morally and physically, thus making them vulnerable to small-scale military operations whose broader destructive effects could be kept tightly in check. The contrast with the contemporary French experience in Indo-China could not be more stark. Two aspects are worth highlighting.

The first contrast derives from Malaya's geographic isolation, which left the MCP entirely dependent on the impoverished local population. To this must be added the unusual circumstance that the insurgents were nearly all members of an ethnic minority, not fish swimming invisibly in the sea of society. The MCP's narrow constituency might have sufficed in a country brought to the brink of dissolution by high levels of violence, but those levels could not be achieved in Malaya because the necessary means could only have come from outside. Conversely, even if the communists had possessed greater capability to use force against the government, they would have been hard pressed to expand their own social base.

The situation in Indo-China was different. Vietnam's long frontiers allowed the insurgents there to gain access to military resources of a kind that could never have reached Malaya. This in turn made an exclusive reliance upon small unit pacification tactics impossible for the French, who were forced, at least occasionally and usually unexpectedly, to confront well-equipped forces capable of fighting them on equal terms. The crucial engagements of the Indo-China War were pitched battles whose consequences were not subject to amelioration by social engineering of the kind that worked so well in Malaya.

The second contrast has to do with the outlook of the French. Even before the Second World War, the British had grown accustomed to the idea that their overseas possessions were destined for independence. After 1945, they ended up fighting in Malaya and elsewhere less from a desire to cling to power, than from a perceived interest in managing such transitions so as to leave behind a stable and friendly post-colonial regime. The French – most especially the French Army – viewed the recovery of their empire as integral to their own national reconstruction, a proposition embodied in the constitution of the Fourth Republic, which conceived France as the metropolitan centre of a global French Union. In Indo-China the French Army would fight a war of intense ideological commitment, intended not simply to crush the Vietnamese Revolution, but to aid France's moral rearmament following its humiliation by the Germans. This was a fantasy that, remarkably, came to be shared by others, including the United States, which bore most of the expenses for the war because it feared the

Ho Chi Minh (right) and Vo Nguyen Giap studying a map in 1950. Their thirty-year collaboration was the beating heart of the Vietnamese revolution. Among civil–military partnerships, only Bismarck and Moltke compare.

consequences of a French defeat, not just in Asia but in Europe. Later on, when it became popular to speak of the countries of Southeast Asia as 'dominoes', few remembered that the last domino was supposed to be France.

The French had been involved in Indo-China as missionaries since the seventeenth century. Traders followed in the eighteenth, garrisons in the nineteenth, by which time French interests had spread throughout the three regions of modern Vietnam – Tonkin in the north, Annam along the central coast, Cochin-China in the south – as well as Laos and Cambodia. At the turn of the twentieth century Annam, Tonkin, Laos and Cambodia were French protectorates, while Cochin-China was a colony subject to direct rule. As elsewhere, proto-nationalist opposition movements arose in response to the French presence. Of these the most important were the Vietnamese communists. Their leading figure was Ho Chi Minh, who first appeared on the world stage as a delegate to the Versailles conference in 1919, where he sought unsuccessfully to advance his homeland's claim to national self-determination under the terms of Woodrow Wilson's Fourteen Points. Ho played a part in founding the French Communist Party in 1920, and spent most of the years between the world wars as a revolutionary organizer, first in the Soviet Union and then in China.

After the fall of France, he was joined in China by Vietnamese nationalists of every stripe, driven out of their own country by the Japanese. Japan's position in Indo-China was more equivocal than in the rest of Southeast Asia, arising not from conquest but from the forcible co-optation of the French administration, which continued to operate under Japanese auspices until the last few months of the war. As elsewhere, they were soon engaged by native guerrillas, backed by the expatriate activists who had taken refuge in China. Their organization, known as the League for the Independence of Vietnam, Viet Minh for short, was not overtly communist, but mirrored the united front adopted by the Kuomintang and the CCP in 1937. Its most effective members were communists, however, including the man responsible for leading the military effort against the Japanese, Vo Nguyen Giap. When the war in Asia ended, Giap's cadres were well-established throughout Tonkin.

By then, conditions in Vietnam had reached a level of complexity that almost beggars description. In March 1945, Japanese forces, fearing an American invasion from the Philippines, took direct control in Indo-China. In Vietnam a puppet government was set up in Saigon under the titular Vietnamese emperor, Bao Dai, who had remained in Vietnam during the war. French garrisons that resisted house arrest were dealt with ferociously. One that escaped into China was interned by Chinese Nationalists acting on American instructions, America being ill-disposed towards French imperialism. The Viet Minh, who appeared no different to the Japanese than other nationalist movements with which they had co-operated, stepped into the resulting

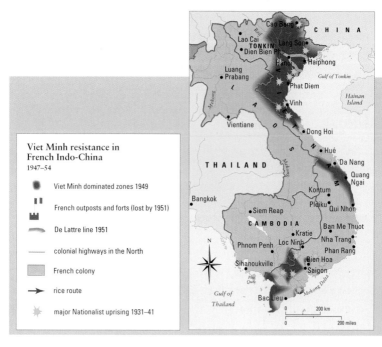

Viet Minh resistance in French Indo-China 1947–54

- Viet Minh dominated zones 1949
- French outposts and forts (lost by 1951)
- De Lattre line 1951
- colonial highways in the North
- French colony
- rice route
- major Nationalist uprising 1931–41

THE FRENCH INDO-CHINA WAR 1947–54

Vietnam is a country just over half the size of France, with a shoreline as long as the west coast of the United States. The interior is mountainous, triple-canopy jungle. Most Vietnamese live along the coast and in the river deltas. Like the Americans later on, the French struggled to reconcile the need to control remote interior areas, in order to disrupt the enemy's command and communications, with the problem of protecting the population itself. The French fought their Vietnam war mainly in the North, an option denied their American successors. It did them no good.

administrative vacuum in Tonkin. Bao Dai did not seek to interfere. The Viet Minh were also supported by the Americans, whose access to information in the region had depended on Free French agents who had been locked up along with their Vichy counterparts. Thus, for a few months in the summer of 1945, Ho's movement found itself enjoying simultaneously cordial relations with the Chinese communists, the Kuomintang, the United States, the emperor of Vietnam, and Japan.

It was not an arrangement destined to last. In August, Japanese troops north of the 16th Parallel surrendered to Chinese Nationalist

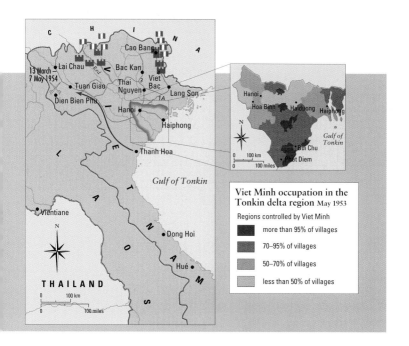

Viet Minh occupation in the Tonkin delta region May 1953

Regions controlled by Viet Minh

- more than 95% of villages
- 70–95% of villages
- 50–70% of villages
- less than 50% of villages

forces, whose interest in plundering the country consumed whatever energy might have been devoted to hampering the expansion of Viet Minh control. The Democratic Republic of Vietnam was proclaimed on 2 September, based in Hanoi and headed by Ho, with symbolic participation by Bao Dai and other non-communist nationalists. To the south, however, the Japanese surrendered to British troops flown in from Burma. British instinct and policy favoured the restoration of the colonial authority, whose representative, General Philippe Leclerc de Hauteclocque, reached Saigon in October. He was joined a month later by Admiral Thierry d'Argenlieu, the new High Commissioner for Indo-China. By the start of 1946, French control south of the 16th Parallel was relatively secure. Likewise in Cambodia, which had also declared independence in March 1945, but was persuaded by Leclerc to accept autonomous status within a still somewhat notional Indo-Chinese Federation, itself an element of the French Union.

A similar solution would be attempted in Vietnam. For leverage, the French had mainly their ability to bring pressure on the Chinese to pull out their troops. In March, it was agreed that these would be replaced by smaller French garrisons, to be withdrawn within five years. In the meantime, Vietnam would accept autonomy on the Cambodian model. It seemed a high price, which Ho was prepared to pay because, as he said, the last time the Chinese came they stayed a thousand years, whereas the French were bound to leave eventually. There is little evidence that either side regarded the arrangement as anything other than a means to buy time. It did not buy much. Even as French troops were returning to Tonkin, d'Argenlieu set about reorganizing Cochin-China as a separate colony. The Viet Minh responded with a campaign of terror, never entirely absent from the scene in any case. Follow-up talks begun in May outside Paris broke down, and after Ho returned to Vietnam hostilities escalated. In November, the French tried to gain control of the customs service in Haiphong, which they had bargained away in their talks with Ho. Their goal was to curtail the smuggling of weapons by Giap. Five days of hard fighting followed, during which French warships and artillery shelled the city. The Viet Minh tried to reply with a general uprising, failed, then withdrew to their wartime bases to wage guerrilla war.

The next three years were a stalemate. The French built up their armed forces, and regained control of Laos by pushing out the Chinese Nationalists and Red guerrillas who had had condominium there since the war. A new government headed by Bao Dai was set up in April 1949. Vietnam became an Associated State of the French Union, independent except in matters involving state finance and national defence. Not everyone found this convincing. The Viet Minh worked to expand their base areas. In military terms, neither side can be said to have made much progress. This was a bad sign for the French. How bad only became apparent in the autumn of 1949, when the communist victory in China transformed the situation in Tonkin. Ho called for general mobilization, and the war entered a new phase.

Tactically, the most critical terrain in northern Vietnam is a 70-mile-long ridge running along the north-east frontier between Cao Bang and

Lang Son. The road atop the ridge is the main transportation corridor north of the Red River delta, and its possession is vital to securing, or interdicting, communications with China. The French position there consisted of five fortified outposts, strung together like beads, and held collectively by about 10,000 men. Even before China fell to the communists, doubts had been raised within the French General Staff about the defensibility of this cordon. In May, the middle outpost of the five, at Dong Khé, was briefly seized by the Viet Minh, only to be retaken a few days later by French paratroops. It was a demonstration of French tactical proficiency that would often be repeated in the next few years; yet puzzling in its way, since if the position was worth retaking so brilliantly it should also have been worth a more concerted defence. None was provided, and after the summer rains subsided the Viet Minh struck again with forces now doubled in size, and equipped for the first time with artillery and mortars. Dong Khé fell in two days. With that, the entire outpost line collapsed in disarray.

This result produced strong reactions on both sides. The French dispatched one of their most talented soldiers, General Jean de Lattre de Tassigny, to take charge of what had suddenly become a desperate struggle. Giap overreached himself. Having beaten one battalion with eight at Dong Khé, he now threw 22,000 men against 6,000 at Vinh Yen, a crossroads north of Hanoi. The attack failed amid heavy casualties from French air strikes. Two months later, in March 1951, he tried again at Mao Khe, north of Haiphong, and was again beaten back. In all, Giap lost about 20,000 men before the summer rains came, a disaster that temporarily restored the initiative to the French.

De Lattre set about building what became known as the De Lattre Line, a ring of watchtowers and blockhouses constructed every mile or so along the perimeter of the Red River delta. Despite appearances, its purpose was offensive: by fortifying what was left of the French base in Tonkin, de Lattre hoped to conserve forces for use in mobile operations. He also sought to mobilize the Vietnamese. It was only in the summer of 1951 that conscription was introduced in Vietnam, a telling reflection of the tenuous nature of Bao Dai's regime. It is also revealing of larger strategic realities. When the fighting turned serious in Indo-China, French forces there numbered about 150,000, more than half of whom were Foreign Legionnaires or colonial troops raised outside France. This number could not be significantly increased. French public opinion was divided about the Indo-China War, and would not support sending French conscripts overseas. This limitation was reinforced by the policy of the United States, which did not regard the containment of communism and the defence of the French empire as synonymous. American aid was dependent to some extent on the adoption of a policy intended to leave Vietnam militarily self-sufficient when the war ended. A division of labour therefore emerged, to be reproduced during the later American war as well, whereby the maintenance of static defences and local security were to be left to Vietnamese troops, while the French took the fight to the enemy.

Major engagements in Indo-China following the failure of Giap's Red River Offensive – as his precipitate rush upon Hanoi and Haiphong has come to be known – arose from efforts by the French to project power beyond the De Lattre Line. Their aim was to lure the Viet Minh into some kind of set-piece battle in which superior French firepower could be decisive; and also to establish strong, remote positions from which French influence could osmose into the countryside, a process commonly compared to the spreading of ink blots. The first attempt produced representative results. In November 1951, three parachute battalions were dropped on the town of Hoa Binh, 25 miles west of the De Lattre Line. A month later, Giap brought six divisions – his entire regular force – against this exposed redoubt, three directly, three against the shoulders of its communications along the Black River. Fighting lasted until February. In the end the paratroops at Hoa Binh were rescued by a column of French infantry, which fought its way back and forth along the main road from Hanoi. Both sides suffered about 5,000 casualties, and the French were back where they were.

The most famous battle fought anywhere since 1945 occurred two years later at Dien Bien Phu. Apart from its scale – Dien Bien Phu was defended by twelve battalions rather than three – and the epic heroism of its defence – there would be no rescue this time – it was little different from Hoa Binh. In the interval, the military balance on the ground had shifted against the French. Chinese aid to Ho's government grew as the Korean War wound down, which accounts for the enormous preponderance of artillery on the communist side at Dien Bien Phu. Some of the guns were manned by Chinese crews. The French appealed for American intervention. A quick Pentagon study concluded that three tactical nuclear weapons, 'properly employed', would suffice to relieve the besieged garrison. These Eisenhower declined to provide, taking refuge in the need for Congressional approval and British consent.

French paratroops arriving at Dien Bien Phu. The hills in the distance would soon bristle with Viet Minh guns, after which high-altitude air drops became the only means to supply the garrison. As the defensive perimeter narrowed, much of what was intended for the French would fall quite literally into enemy hands.

Even had it been won, the battle of Dien Bien Phu would have been an empty exercise for the French, who had already agreed to negotiations that could only result in a partition like the one already in place in Korea. The conference that was destined to reach this conclusion was already under way in Geneva when the siege ended on 7 May 1954. Two months later, Vietnam was partitioned at the 17th Parallel. Ho's government would prevail in the North, while a separate republic would rule in the South, headed by one of Bao Dai's lieutenants, Ngo Dinh Diem. National elections to unify the country were scheduled for 1956. Laos and Cambodia became independent monarchies. The United States had publicly ruled out intervention in Indo-China if the conference failed. Yet it remained frustrated by the equivocal results of its efforts to contain communism in Asia, and stated, once the proceedings had ended, that while it would abide by the agreements reached, it would view any renewal of aggression with grave concern.

DIEN BIEN PHU

In a remote valley, Dien Bien Phu was intended to be re-supplied entirely from the air. Its airstrip was closed almost immediately by shellfire from surrounding hills. Base defences were organized around a system of strong points: Huguette, Dominique, Eliane and Claudine formed the central position; Béatrice, Ann-Marie and Gabrielle lay 1 1/2 miles to the north, with Isabelle 4 miles to the south.

1. 20 November 1953: French parachute landings begin, eventually driving out the defending Viet Minh, one battalion of 148th Infantry Regiment

2. General Giap orders his forces to isolate the French position and to close on Dien Bien Phu, initially the 308th and 312th Divisions with supporting troops

3. The French decide to hold at all costs, and pull back troops from outlying areas to concentrate on Dien Bien Phu

4. 13 March 1954: the full Viet Minh assault begins, attacking Gabrielle and Béatrice outposts. Béatrice fell on 13 March and Gabrielle on 15 March. Viet Minh artillery now covered the airfield and French re-supply could now only be by parachute

5. The northern outpost of Anne-Marie fell on 17 March. After a lull in the fighting the attacks continued on 30 March settling down to a classic siege, digging mines and approach trenches

6. 1 May: the final phase of Viet Minh attacks begins. By 7 May it was all over. The Viet Minh had lost some 8,000 plus killed, many more wounded. Meanwhile the French and their local allies lost 2,000 killed, 6,500 wounded and 10,000 captured

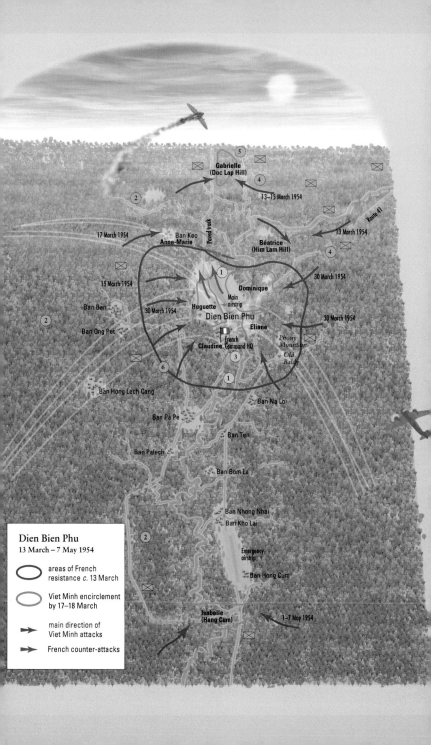

Gabrielle
(Doc Lap Hill)
5
4
13–15 March 1954

Route 41

2

17 March 1954
Ban Keo
Anne-Marie
Forest track
Béatrice
(Him Lam Hill)
13 March 1954
4

1
Dominique
30 March 1954
15 March 1954
Main
airstrip
Huguette
Dien Bien Phu
30 March 1954
Ban Ban
2
Ban Ong Pet
Eliane
30 March 1954
Phony
Mountain
Claudine Command HQ
French
3
Old
Baldy
6
1

Ban Hong Lech Cang
Ban Na Loi

Ban Pá Pé

Ban Ten

Ban Palech

Ban Bom La

Ban Nhong Nhai
Ban Kho Lai

2

Emergency
airstrip

Ban Hong Cum

Dien Bien Phu
13 March – 7 May 1954

⬭ areas of French
resistance *c.* 13 March

⬭ Viet Minh encirclement
by 17–18 March

➤ main direction of
Viet Minh attacks

➤ French counter-attacks

Isabelle
(Hang Cum)
1–7 May 1954

CHAPTER FOUR

Algeria

An Algerian soldier guards FLN prisoners. Revolutionary wars are almost always civil wars as well. As many native Algerians took up arms for the French as for the National Liberation Front. Tens of thousands paid with their lives after the French left.

Algeria

In war, morale and public opinion comprise the better part of
reality.

Napoleon

THE SECOND WORLD WAR in Europe ended on 7 May 1945. The
next day, VE Day, a public ceremony was planned at Sétif, in
Algeria. When Algerian nationalists used the occasion to protest the
arrest of one of their leaders the police tried to confiscate their banners.
Riot followed, then massacre, which went on for five days. One
hundred and three Europeans were killed, often atrociously. Then the
army moved in to restore calm, a task that led to another 500 deaths,
Muslims now. Many were killed by dive-bombers and naval gunfire.
Over the next few weeks reprisals by European colonists would total
another 6,000 dead.

The events at Sétif precede the start of the Algerian Revolution by
nine years. Yet they already capture most of its essential elements,
above all an astounding propensity for atavistic violence. There have
been few conflicts of similar scale and consequence – few, at any rate,
involving a Western army – in which terror, assassination, torture,
mutilation, random slaughter, hostage taking and summary executions
have played such a preponderant role. This is obviously a relative
judgement. These tactics stand out in Algeria not because they are
uniquely present, but because more organized forms of fighting are
largely absent. Algeria's National Liberation Front (FLN) rarely
possessed the means to conduct sustained operations of any scale.
They succeeded despite their limited resources because their adversaries
were repeatedly reduced to fighting fire with fire, a disastrous tendency
that finally ruined them.

Sétif also reveals the complex social geography of the Algerian war,
in which there were three sides: the French government; the Algerian
nationalists; and Algeria's European settlers, called *pieds noirs*, or

'black feet'. Their equivocal position is revealed by the competing etymologies that attach to this name. Among Muslims, it was supposed to refer to the Europeans' black leather shoes. To metropolitan Frenchmen, it signified the settlers' sunburned feet. There were a million *pieds noirs* in Algeria in 1950, living in the cities and the fertile coastal plain, alongside nine million Arab and Berber Muslims. Only one in five were of French descent, the rest being Spanish, Italian, Corsican, Maltese, and so on. All, however, were French citizens, Algeria being legally part of France, no different than Provence or Burgundy as far as its white inhabitants were concerned. The Algerian Revolution was fought to a finish because the *pieds noirs* refused to countenance any solution that would leave them on equal terms with their Muslim neighbours. It reacted disastrously upon the politics of France itself because French public opinion was divided by the brutality of the repression carried out in its name, and because significant elements of the French Army backed the *pieds noirs* in defiance of their own government.

French Legionnaires check the identity papers of a group of nomads.

Sétif was an important step in the progress of Algerian nationalism, of which there were three basic streams. The oldest, the Ulema, sought to resist French influence by promoting strict Islamic observance. A second movement, the most influential before the war, was the UDMA (Union Démocratique pour le Manifeste Algérien). It favoured Algerian legal and civil equality with the rest of France, but not separation from it. After Sétif, it and the moderate programme it represented would gradually be cast into the shade by a group know in 1945 as the MTLD (Movement pour le Triomphe de Libertés Démocratiques). It shared the Islamist values of the Ulema, but combined them with a conventionally leftist social agenda. The MTLD demanded complete independence from France. It was the imprisonment of its leader, Messali Hadj, that had sparked the Sétif demonstration. From it would grow the FLN, a clandestine splinter group committed to direct action, which would make the Algerian Revolution. The French Army, tasked with crushing it, always insisted it was fighting communism in Algeria. It wasn't. The Algerian Communist Party (PCA) distrusted the Islamic religiosity of the nationalists, and declared the Sétif uprising to be the work of fascists. Although the PCA would eventually be co-opted by the FLN, its members never played a leading role.

The FLN was an underground organization, not a mass movement. Its violence was directed primarily at the Muslim population, which it sought to radicalize by persuasion and terror. Attacks on *pieds noirs* were also important, of course, and reliably provocative. Sétif revealed the extraordinary reaction that attacks against European civilians would inspire, which in turn became a reason to carry them out, since the indiscriminate repression that followed would further destabilize the status quo. Nevertheless, if the FLN lacked the social base necessary to wage a people's war on the Maoist model, it undoubtedly rested upon a mass phenomenon, namely the contempt with which Algeria's Europeans viewed their Muslim countrymen. Jules Roy, a *pieds noirs* who wrote a good account of the war, was ashamed to recall that the one thing everyone knew about Arabs was that their happiness was elsewhere, rather, if you please, like the happiness of cattle. 'They don't have the same needs we do,' I was always being told. I was glad to believe it, and from that moment on their condition could not disturb me. Who suffers seeing oxen sleep on straw or eating grass?

To this must be added economic hardship, brought on by population pressure, the concentration of land ownership in settler hands and the general deterioration of material conditions that accompanied the world wars. In 1955 the average personal income of Algerian Muslims was one-thirtieth that of their European counterparts. Their political resignation was symptomatic of deprivation and despair, which the FLN would exploit with violence and cunning.

On 1 November 1954, Algeria was beset by a wave of attacks on French military and police, public buildings, settler property and Muslims associated with the French administration. Except for their number – about sixty altogether – these episodes were not categorically distinguishable from similar disturbances that had punctuated Algerian life for years. Many failed, or suffered heavy casualties because the police had been tipped off. It was nevertheless the beginning of a co-ordinated attempt at insurrection. Planning had begun in the spring, at the time of Dien Bien Phu, which the FLN leadership saw as opening a window of opportunity. The attacks were accompanied by a broadcast on Cairo radio calling on Algerians to rise in the cause of freedom, and upon world opinion to see the justice of their actions.

French reaction was adamantine. France's Premier, Pierre Mendès-France, a socialist and a hero of the Resistance, declared that Algeria was part of France, and would remain such. His intention was to seek peace by hastening Algeria's integration with France, on terms designed to improve the position of the Muslims. This policy was acceptable to neither the *pieds noirs* nor the FLN. It was, in any case, dependent upon the restoration of order, for which purpose additional military forces were sent, including some of the toughest units in the French

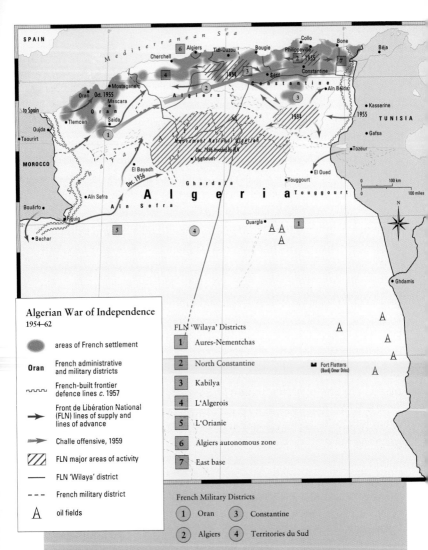

Algerian War of Independence
1954–62

- areas of French settlement

- **Oran** — French administrative and military districts

- French-built frontier defence lines *c.* 1957

- Front de Libération National (FLN) lines of supply and lines of advance

- Challe offensive, 1959

- FLN major areas of activity

- FLN 'Wilaya' district

- French military district

- $\mathbb{A}$ oil fields

FLN 'Wilaya' Districts

1. Aures-Nementchas
2. North Constantine
3. Kabilya
4. L'Algerois
5. L'Oranie
6. Algiers autonomous zone
7. East base

French Military Districts

1. Oran
2. Algiers
3. Constantine
4. Territories du Sud

ALGERIAN WAR OF INDEPENDENCE 1954–62

French rule in Algeria was exercised through four military districts, whose co-operation was often imperfect. The FLN established their own shadow government based on seven 'Wilaya', designed to cut across French administrative boundaries. Wilaya 3, in the mountains of Kabilya, was their last redoubt.

Army, recently returned from Indo-China. By February, three members of the nine-member FLN executive were dead or in jail, and a campaign of collective reprisal was under way in the Constantine, where the FLN was strongest. It struck back in August 1955 at Philippeville, where 123 Europeans and Muslims were systematically murdered, the Muslims by having their throats cut in the manner traditionally used to butcher sheep. Estimates of those killed in the punitive campaign that followed range from 1,200 to 12,000.

Philippeville accelerated the French military build-up, and shifted its emphasis towards local security. A system called *quadrillage* was instituted that sought to maintain a uniform military presence throughout the country, a difficult feat, but possible because, in contrast to Indo-China, there was no prohibition on the employment of French conscripts in Algeria. *Quadrillage* also included provisions for resettling suspect populations, plus special units, led by Arabic-speaking officers, that worked to promote economic development and ameliorate grievances. With conscripts and Muslim auxiliaries filling the security role, paratroops and Legionnaires employing helicopters and air strikes were free to root out organized FLN units, now known as the Armée de libération nationale (ALN). Such methods achieved a good deal, to judge by the damage they inflicted. Although ALN numbers increased along with the general level of violence, casualties kept up. Almost 14,000 ALN fighters were killed in 1956, well over half its effective strength. At the same time, total French forces in Algeria approached 500,000.

The rising pressure inspired the FLN to increase its efforts to secure outside assistance. From the start, two members of the FLN leadership group, Ahmed Ben Bella and Mohamed Khider, had been based in Cairo. Their presence reflected the (misplaced) hopes vested in Egypt's pan-Arabist President, Gamal Abdel Nasser, who was himself embroiled with the French over control of the Suez Canal. In October 1956, Nasser finally acceded to Ben Bella's pleading, and put together a

Ahmed Ben Bella, one of the FLN's founding fathers, and Algeria's first president. Ben Bella spent most of the war in a French prison, after a plane in which he was flying was hijacked by French intelligence. His long captivity made him a symbol of Algerian intransigence, and French intransigence as well.

boatload of weapons, which was intercepted by the French Navy. The loss was sorely felt, for although the cargo amounted to only 70 tons of small arms, mortars and ammunition, it may well have exceeded the total arsenal of the ALN at that moment. Its discovery infuriated the French, who had long had an exaggerated impression of Nasser's contribution to the Algerian war. Retaliation followed eight days later, when an Air Maroc plane departing Cairo for Tunis was diverted to Algeria. On board were Ben Bella, Khider and several other members of the FLN Cairo bureau, all of whom were locked up in France. This action, an intelligence coup by any standard, was equally a gross violation of international law, against which world opinion reacted strongly. It would soon have worse to contemplate.

Like all major episodes of the Algerian war, the events that became known as the Battle of Algiers arose from a series of escalating reprisals, which began with the execution of two FLN terrorists in June 1956. Dozens of Europeans were shot down at random in revenge, to which *pieds noirs* vigilantes replied by planting explosives around FLN safe houses in the Casbah. Eighty people died when these went off. An FLN bombing campaign followed, carried out, famously, by young Muslim women masquerading as Europeans. This escalatory pattern should not be mistaken for spontaneous rage. Hard-pressed in the hinterlands, the FLN turned its attention to Algiers because its densely packed Muslim population and rabbit-warren landscape offered some refuge from the methods that were defeating it elsewhere. Once the Casbah was revolutionized, it was supposed to become the base from which new operations could be launched. Taking the war to the capital was also intended to attract the attention of the world: many a bomb can explode in the countryside with no one the wiser. It was a decision that most insurgencies confront at some point: when to move against the cities. Cities hold unique perils, not least a heightened risk of being observed and betrayed. The urban guerrilla, even more than his rural counterpart, must be a face in a crowd. Against an adversary willing to deal ruthlessly with the crowd, this can be a dangerous position.

In December, the mayor of Algiers was murdered in broad daylight, and elements of the élite 10th Parachute Division were called in to restore order by any means necessary. Prominent among these would be the use of torture to extract information from prisoners. Torture allowed the French to build up an exact model of the FLN organization in Algiers, and to obtain information quickly enough for it still to be useful in responding to FLN attacks. Many victims simply disappeared, but not all, since intimidation was part of the point. Besides, the 10th Paras' formidable commander, Jacques Massu, was not prepared to apologize for methods he regarded as having been imposed by the inhuman practices of the enemy – among which Massu seems personally to have been most offended by the practice of mutilating or castrating Muslims who violated Islamic law by smoking cigarettes, drinking wine and so on. By the end of September, the FLN in Algiers was shattered. Saadi Yacef, architect of the uprising, was betrayed by a tortured bomb courier and taken alive. The famous desperado Ali la Pointe, who had killed the mayor, was blown up, along with the building he was hiding in, after he refused to surrender.

Massu's victory shaped the remainder of the Algerian war. Although it cannot realistically be said to have made the conflict more brutal than it already was, it brought that brutality home to the French public in a way that proved especially poisonous. Frenchmen who had lived through the German occupation knew what torture was, and while many accepted the logic of Massu's pragmatic explanation, that did not banish the taste of ashes. The issue also had a rending effect upon the army. Elite professionals like the 10th Paras accepted such methods as part and parcel of what it meant to fight revolutionary war, and viewed the temporizing of civilians as a sign of moral weakness and incipient betrayal. In this connection, Indo-China was much on their minds. Conscripts were more uneasy, which in turn amplified the impact of public revulsion: French parents did not relish the prospect of

their sons attaching electrodes to the genitals of 'suspects', even if the honour of France was stake – itself something of a moot point, under the circumstances. Among the *pieds noirs*, finally, the Battle of Algiers was taken as a signal that the French Army had finally acquired some backbone. They believed victory on their terms was at hand. When they discovered they were wrong, the war would enter a new phase.

The FLN defeat in Algiers was compounded by setbacks elsewhere. In March 1956, France granted independence to its protectorates in Tunisia and Morocco, Algeria's neighbours to the east and west. Neither was eager for conflict with France. Yet the kidnapping of Ben Bella – who had, after all, been on a Moroccan plane bound for

Legionnaire paratroops deploying from a helicopter. The Algerian war was the first in which helicopters were routinely used to provide tactical mobility and logistics. The French could hardly have controlled the Algerian countryside without them. The precedent weighed heavily with the United States, which employed similar methods, less successfully, in Vietnam.

Tunis – was sufficiently offensive that afterwards both were prepared to provide unofficial sanctuary to ALN troops. Algeria's revolutionaries thus acquired one of the most characteristic and valuable resources of successful insurgencies: base areas protected by international frontiers. The French reacted by establishing impregnable cordon defences on both borders, stretching from the Mediterranean to the wastes of the Sahara. The fortifications on the Tunisian side, called the Morice Line after the incumbent Minister of Defence, were the most imposing, because of Tunisia's critical position on the flank of the FLN stronghold in the Constantine. The central feature was an 8-foot-high fence electrified to 5,000 volts, surrounded by landmines and patrolled by forces totalling 80,000 men.

No significant ALN forces ever crossed the Morice Line, but they did continue to build up behind it, a large and increasingly well-equipped conventional force that cast an ominous shadow over the French counter-insurgency effort. Although it is unlikely that the ALN regulars massing in Tunisia could have defeated the French Army, they constituted a stronger force than any the French had faced so far. Their existence came to symbolize the irreducible nature of the FLN challenge: what must the state of Algerian opinion be before the Morice Line could be safely dismantled? Simply to put the question in this way reveals how parlous the French political position had become, despite every appearance of victory inside Algeria itself.

The Morice Line became the scene of an incident that further heightened international concern about French conduct, and indirectly set great events in motion. In February 1958, a French reconnaissance plane was shot down by fire from a Tunisian village called Sakiet, across the border from an area where a French patrol had been ambushed. The French protested to Tunis, and then, following another attack a few days later, levelled the village with air strikes. Tunisia protested to the UN Security Council, two of whose members, the United States and Great Britain, now offered to mediate the dispute – the first formal sign that France's 'internal' conflict with

A French outpost in the Atlas Mountains. Geologically, the Atlas are an extension of the European Alps. Their arid side marks the beginning of the Sahara, which, when not unbearably hot, is unbearably cold.

Algeria was ceasing to be regarded as such by its important allies. To the dismay of the army, the *pieds noirs* and the French Right, the French Premier, Félix Gaillard, accepted. In so doing, he took the opportunity to disavow the Sakiet attack, which he declared had been carried out by the army on its own authority.

In April, Gaillard's government fell amidst the resulting uproar. In the weeks necessary to form a new one, conditions in Algeria reached a breaking point. The last straw was provided by the FLN, which announced on 9 May that it had executed three French soldiers for the crimes of murder, rape and torture. The French commander in Algiers, Raoul Salan, notified Paris of the executions, and also that the army would not tolerate any government that would abandon Algeria. Four days later, at a ceremony honouring the dead soldiers, 20,000 *pieds noirs* poured into the streets, demanding that the army seize power. Massu, summoned by the crowd, constituted a Committee of Public Safety, to which Salan allowed himself to be named. Later, he and Massu would threaten military action against France, unless a 'national arbiter' was appointed to form 'a government of public safety'.

The arbiter they had in mind was Charles de Gaulle, a wanderer in the political wilderness since 1946, when he resigned the leadership of France's first post-war government, rather than brook continued opposition from the Left. Support for de Gaulle's return had been brewing for months before the *pied noir* uprising brought matters to a head. His position in French politics was unique. A hero to the officer corps, he was widely viewed even by the Left as a man beyond parties. He was swept to power on 1 June 1958, because he enjoyed the confidence of the army, and also because those who feared the army thought he was the only man in France who could stave off a *coup d'état*. His mandate was to rule by decree for six months, and then present a new constitution to replace the discredited Fourth Republic. Three days later he went to Algiers, and told a mixed crowd of *pieds noirs*, soldiers, and Muslims that 'I have understood you'. Everyone thought he was talking to them.

De Gaulle's policy on Algeria was in fact a mystery, and an old one. As leader of the Free French, de Gaulle had convened a conference of French colonial administrators at Brazzaville in January 1944. Its published proceedings included a forceful statement by de Gaulle's commissioner for colonies, ruling out 'all idea of [colonial] autonomy, all possibility of an evolution outside the French bloc of empire', and rejecting 'even the distant establishment of self-government'. It also contained an eloquent statement by de Gaulle himself, affirming his intention 'to lead each of the colonial peoples to a development that will permit them to administer themselves, and, later, to govern themselves'. Nothing had happened since then to resolve these contradictions. On the contrary, they had been cultivated with a view to preserving freedom of action. In reality, de Gaulle's preferred outcome was no different from that of Mendès-France, Gaillard, and every government in between: Algeria as France's partner, on something approaching equal terms. The difference was that de Gaulle's personal standing would allow him to cut his losses if the circle could not be squared. His aim was to save Algeria for France. Failing that, he would save France.

Militarily, conditions in Algeria had reached the crux. Driven out of the cities, and contained by the border cordons, the FLN seemed ripe for final destruction. The instrument for accomplishing it was Maurice Challe, an Air Force general sent to relieve the politically suspect Salan. Challe reorganized French forces to create a mobile reserve of two divisions, backed by Muslim auxiliaries whose numbers now reached 60,000. With these he would sweep across Algeria from west to east, rooting out the ALN guerrillas and driving them against the Morice Line. By the autumn of 1959, organized resistance was confined to the remote regions of the Aures Mountains. Challe, preparing to mop up, declared the military phase of the rebellion over. The FLN leadership, defiant, announced the formation of a government in exile.

Less than three years later they would return to Algiers at the head of a new national government. The proximate cause of this remarkable reversal was the intensifying crisis in French civil–military relations, which drove events in the last years of the war. But this should not obscure the nature of the FLN's achievement, at what proved to be its nadir. It had set out to render Algeria ungovernable by France, and it had succeeded. This did not by itself ensure the FLN's ascendancy, but it did rule out any compromise that would have been remotely acceptable to the *pieds noirs* and their supporters in the French Army. French military success had left these groups with the initiative, which they would now use to effect their own destruction.

The push that sent events out of control came from de Gaulle, who regarded Challe's offensive not as a bid for outright victory, but as a means of creating favourable conditions for a negotiated settlement. In September, he announced that the moment had come for 'recourse to self-determination' in Algeria – a phrase of calculated ambiguity that certainly did not correspond to what Challe and his fellow officers thought they were fighting for. Challe declared that he could not ask soldiers to die except to keep Algeria part of France. With this as their cue, *pieds noirs* extremists organized themselves into the French National Front (FNF), to which tinder a match was set by Massu. He told a German journalist that most French officers would no longer unconditionally obey de Gaulle's orders. Massu was relieved of his command, and the FNF called a general strike in Algiers. A large crowd assembled, and when police tried to disperse it, violence erupted in which fourteen policemen were killed. The French Army temporized, insisting that Frenchman could not fire upon Frenchman – a thought that had evidently not occurred to the FNF. Barricades were thrown up, which stood for a week before being abandoned, more from a desire to get out of the rain than from any action by Challe's troops.

European women bring provisions to pieds noirs partisans during Barricades Week in January 1960. Although the French Army has had a lot of experience demolishing barricades since 1789, local commanders in Algiers refused to fire on white settlers. Eventually, inclement weather sufficed to clear the streets.

Secret talks with the FLN got under way shortly thereafter. Progress was halting owing to fierce factionalism on the Algerian side – in its way a mirror image of what the French were experiencing. Throughout the war, the FLN leadership had been dispersed within and beyond Algeria. With the prospect of success before their eyes, personal and political rivalries grew more intense. Those who had remained inside Algeria were, understandably, more conciliatory in their outlook. Yet they were blamed by their colleagues in Tunis and Cairo for the disaster of the Challe offensive, and lost influence as a result. Some were executed for attempting to reach out to the French on their own. By the time public talks got under way, in June 1960, the hard-liners were in control, and negotiations broke down over their insistence that nothing could be done until Ben Bella, still languishing in a French jail, was released. The next month, FLN terrorism in Algeria began to revive, a predictable consequence of the inactivity of the French Army which was now neither willing, nor trusted, to carry out significant operations.

The words 'Algerian republic' first passed de Gaulle's lips in a speech on 4 November, announcing a referendum on Algerian 'self-determination', to be conducted simultaneously in both Algeria and France. A month later he returned to Algeria for a final effort at conciliation. He took his life in his hands – four assassination attempts miscarried – and left havoc in his wake, as the worst rioting in years engulfed Algiers and Oran. The referendum, held in January 1961, was in effect a mandate to resume negotiations. It passed with 75 per cent of the vote, though four in ten Muslims stayed away. Among the *pieds noirs*, 72 per cent voted no.

Resistance within the French Army now reached its culminating point, in the form of an ill-conceived attempt to take over the government in Algiers. The effort was led by Challe, embittered at the thought of abandoning loyal Muslim troops to a grim fate should the FLN take charge. Challe intended nothing more than an emphatic gesture, sufficient to bring down de Gaulle and impose a new policy. Others envisioned themselves carving a new life out of an Arabinfested wilderness, and joining the UN. Still others imagined a march on Paris. All, however, miscalculated the state of mind of the majority of French troops, who despite everything remained loyal to legitimately constituted authority. Only one regiment of Legionnaire paratroops supported the coup unreservedly; and while some 14,000 individuals were eventually implicated, that was too few in an army of half a million. In some cases, officers who stood with the plotters were simply arrested by the conscripts they commanded.

In political terms, the failure of the army coup in April 1961 was the last measure of disillusion necessary for de Gaulle to move forward. Given the obvious stakes for France, significant concessions would now be acceptable if it meant being rid of the Algerian war. At the same time, however, France's military weakness created scant incentives for the FLN to make concessions of its own. Negotiations dragged on for almost a year, preoccupied by questions about who would control oil wells, naval bases and rocket test-sites in the Sahara. As they did, a final spasm of violence enveloped the scene.

The instigator was the OAS (Organisation Armée Secrète), the most lethal of all the groups born from the rage of the pieds noirs and the disaffection of the army. Originally intent upon a campaign of assassination – its highest aspiration was to kill de Gaulle – the OAS saw its numbers swell in the aftermath of the failed coup in April. Its programme expanded accordingly. In the second half of 1961, the OAS conducted an average of 3,000 terrorist attacks per month, including hundreds in France itself, directed at Muslims, French officials, loyal army officers, and white settlers whose views were insufficiently extreme. Its aim was to establish itself as the voice of the *pieds noirs*, and to inspire FLN reprisals on a scale that would require the French Army to reassert control in defiance of civilian restraint from Paris. The FLN responded as expected, while the French Army defended itself against all comers, often with considerable force, qualms about firing on Frenchmen having long since been set aside.

The tripartite struggle between the FLN, the OAS and the French

Army lasted until the summer of 1962. It was the most intense fighting of the war. The French Army suffered 35,000 fatalities from all causes during the Algerian Revolution. Half came between the failed coup of April 1961, and the proclamation of Algerian independence fifteen months later. A similar pattern prevailed on the civilian side. By the spring of 1961, the FLN had killed about 2,700 Europeans and almost 17,000 Muslims. Another 14,000 civilians, nearly all Muslims, had disappeared. During the war's final year, however, another 50,000 would die, a number that would in turn be dwarfed by the 150,000 Muslim loyalists purged by the FLN after it took power. The French Army was obliged to stand by and witness much of this, its hands tied by a ceasefire agreement that became effective in March 1962. Thereafter, French soldiers were not allowed to intervene in the slaughter going on around them. They were also required to disarm and abandon their Muslim auxiliaries, whose escape they were forbidden to aid.

The OAS uprising settled the fate of the *pieds noirs*, though not as intended. The FLN had always proclaimed its willingness to accept Algeria's European inhabitants as citizens, and their right to remain was spelled out in the final peace terms. Over the course of the FLN's confrontation with the OAS, however, its real policy evolved towards what would one day be called 'ethnic cleansing'. By the end of the Algerian war, the choices for the *pieds noirs* had been reduced to 'the coffin or the suitcase'. Nearly all of them left, most with nothing more than what they could carry in their hands.

As for the FLN, its accession to power was followed by the sort of murderous factionalism characteristic of post-revolutionary governments. Never a democratic movement, it did not produce a democratic regime. In the end the key to power proved to be the regular forces of the ALN, drilling and polishing on the Tunisian side of the Morice Line. The ALN was the one intact and functioning institution left in Algeria after 1962. Its commander, Houari Boumedienne, backed Ben Bella's successful bid for power after the war, then took the presidency himself in a military coup three years later. He died in office in 1978.

CHAPTER FIVE

Africa and South Asia

'General China', one of the leaders of the Mau Mau Rebellion in Kenya, on trial for his life. China, whose real name was Waruhio, escaped execution by arranging the surrender of other members of his movement. His striking hairstyle was a Mau Mau trademark.

Africa and South Asia

> National consciousness, instead of being the all-embracing
> crystallization of the innermost hopes of the whole people,
> instead of being the immediate and most obvious result of the
> mobilization of the people, will be in any case only an empty
> shell, a crude and fragile travesty of what it might have been.
> The faults that we find in it are quite sufficient explanation of
> the facility with which, when dealing with young and
> independent nations, the nation is passed over for the race, and
> the tribe is preferred to the state.
>
> *Franz Fanon*, The Wretched of the Earth

IN HUMAN AND geographic terms, the weight of European imperialism in the twentieth century lay in the vast territories of Africa and the Indian subcontinent. When the Second World War ended, only one state in each of these regions was ruled by an unambiguously indigenous authority: Ethiopia, whose ancient royal line had just been restored following the defeat of Italy; and Nepal, whose isolation had spared it formal colonization by the British. Liberia was governed by an oligarchy descended mainly from Americans, Egypt (which still housed a British garrison) by a dynasty founded in 1811 by the Macedonian adventurer, Muhammad Ali. There were also two white settler states: Southern Rhodesia (autonomous under the British crown since 1923) and South Africa. All else was empire, ruled by Europeans directly, or through the co-optation of local élites.

Apart from Algeria, the only states in Africa to achieve independence by waging war against their colonial masters were the former Portuguese colonies of Mozambique, Guinea and Angola. The French colony of Madagascar tried to do so, but failed, and later attained independence by non-violent means. Namibia also fought to free itself from South Africa, which ruled the former German colony under a UN mandate. In Rhodesia, the long and intermittently violent

British mounted policemen dispersing rioters in Calcutta, January 1931. The demonstration marked the release from prison of Mahatma Gandhi. He had been locked up the year before, along with 60,000 other people, for protesting the tax of salt.

campaign for democratic rights by the black majority was as much a struggle for national identity as it was for social equality, a statement that also applies to the effort to overthrow apartheid in South Africa. Elsewhere, nationhood, or its semblance, was achieved either by a negotiated transfer of power, or by token resistance and civil unrest giving a final shove to a colonial regime already on its way out.

Nevertheless, both Africa and South Asia would see more than their share of irredentist and secessionist wars, arising in part from conditions that European imperialism created and left unresolved. In neither region were colonial frontiers drawn with any attention to underlying social or cultural realities. They reflected power relationships among the colonizers, and pushed native peoples together, or apart, in whatever way best suited European strategic and economic interests. Which is not to suggest that, within the framework of the imperial enterprise, some obviously better alternative presented itself. As the belated effort to account for sectarian conflict in Britain's Indian Empire suggests, it was not feasible to cut the cloth intricately enough to satisfy all the native interests involved. Apart from paternalism, the dominant ethos of most colonial regimes was federalism, whereby local differences might be acknowledged, and exploited, within the limits of governmental efficiency. Such arrangements proved ripe for adjustment by force once colonial authority had gone. Although it is scarcely possible to do justice to the innumerable conflicts that have resulted from these conditions, a brief discussion of a few cases may shed a useful light on the meaning and limitations of the national idea in two parts of the world where much was expected of it.

By any reckoning, the stakes after 1945 were highest in India, the second most populous polity on earth. Britain's Indian subjects contributed significantly to the war effort in the First World War – one million Indians served overseas, of whom one in ten became casualties – and they anticipated significant concessions in return. These fell short of what was expected, leading to a progressive radicalization of Indian public life. The watershed was the Amritsar massacre of 1919, in which four hundred unarmed Indians were killed by British soldiers dispersing a nationalist demonstration. Nevertheless, although violent protest was not unknown thereafter, the basic thrust of Indian nationalism between the wars favoured non-violent non-co-operation with authorities. This reflected the influence of the famous pacifist, Mohandas Gandhi, and the palliative effects of political success by the notionally all-Indian Congress Party, which gradually gained administrative control of the subcontinent's provincial governments.

Both the Congress Party and Gandhi's movement represented themselves as secular and national in character. Both, however, were viewed as distinctly Hindu in spirit by India's ethnic and religious minorities, of which the most important were the Muslims, comprising a quarter of the subcontinent's population. The last decades of British rule were marked by rising tension between India's Hindus and Muslims, to which the British responded with reforms intended to ensure the proportional representation of minorities within a federalized colonial government. By the late 1930s, however, a movement for Muslim independence was well established, in opposition to what its proponents saw as the 'Hindu Raj'.

The Hindu Raj did not survive the Second World War, to which India's viceroy committed it without consulting the indigenous political leadership. All of the Congress Party's provincial ministers resigned in protest, an occasion that the leader of India's Muslim League, Mohammed Ali Jinnah, declared a 'day of deliverance' from a collusive, sectarian regime. Nevertheless, even after the war, as Indian independence became a foregone conclusion, the unappeasable reality of Islamic separatism was not generally appreciated. It only became so following the outbreak of widespread unrest in August 1946. When Lord Louis Mountbatten arrived as viceroy seven months later, he concluded that civil war loomed, and forced through a scheme that detached two (disconnected) areas with Muslim majorities, and created from them the state of Pakistan. Once the location of these hastily drawn lines became known, millions of Hindus and Muslims took flight, seeking safety on one side or the other. As many as one million people may have perished in the carnage that accompanied the partition of British India, an episode not of war but of communal massacre and vendetta on an epic scale.

War followed soon enough. Mountbatten's plan applied in the first instance only to provinces ruled directly by Britain. Surrounding

OVERLEAF: BRITISH INDIA

The British Empire in India was comprised of territories roughly thirteen times as large as Britain itself, some ruled directly by the Crown, others by dependent local princes who had become feudatories of the Raj. A hundred thousand or so European soldiers and civilians usually sufficed to control this vast expanse, a tribute, no doubt, to the intelligence, humanity, and guile of both the rulers and the ruled.

RUSSIA

Amu Darya

Faizabad

1963
claimed by India as part of
Kashmir border agreed by
Pakistan and China

1979
Russian invasion of Afghanistan
occupied until 1989

ceasefire line

Herat

AFGHANISTAN

Kabul

1980–88
over 2 million
refugees
1971

Rawalpindi

Indus

Jammu and
Kashmir

0,7

Kandahar

Lahore

Ravi

Amritsar

1965

Himchal
Pradesh

Quetta

Chenab

Punjab
Sikh struggle for
separatist state (Khalistan)

Haryana

4,1

Sutlej

Delhi

0,2

IRAN

PAKISTAN

Pokran
nuclear test centre

5,9

Agra

Ganges

1,2

0,3

Uttar
Prades

1958
Gwadar Omani
ceded to Pakistan

Sind

Hyderabad

Rajasthan

Rana
Pratap
Sagar

Luc

Al

Karachi

TROPIC OF CANCER

1965
Cutch border war
1968
Arbitration

0,7

Gujerat
Kathiawar

Ahmedabad

I N D I A

Bhopal

Madhya Pradesh

Arabian Sea

Diu

Damao

1961
annexed by India
formerly Portuguese

1961
annexed by India
formerly Portuguese

Berar

Nagpur

20°

Bombay

Maharashtra

Hyderabad

Yanam

1961
annexed by India
formerly Portuguese

Goa

Andhra
Pradesh

1954
to India from France

Karnataka

Mangalore

Bangalore

Madras

Mahé

Pondicherry
1954
to India from France

1954
to India from France

Kerala

Tamil
Nadu

Karical 1954
to India from France

*Laccadive
Islands*

Thumba
Vikram
Sarabai

*Gulf of
Mannar*

Palk Strait

1988
Tamil riots and
guerrilla war
Indian intervention

Colombo

Kandy

SRI
LANKA

INDIAN OCEAN

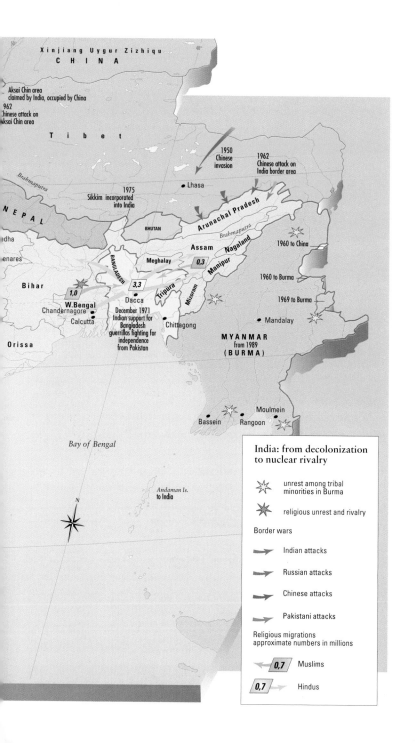

Xinjiang Uygur Zizhiqu
CHINA

Aksai Chin area
claimed by India, occupied by China
1962
Chinese attack on
Aksai Chin area

Tibet

Brahmaputra

1950
Chinese
invasion

1962
Chinese attack on
India border area

● Lhasa

1975
Sikkim incorporated
into India

NEPAL

BHUTAN

Arunachal Pradesh

Brahmaputra

BANGLADESH

Assam

Nagaland

1960 to China

Meghalay

0,3

Manipur

1960 to Burma

edha

enares

Bihar

1,0

W.Bengal

Chandernagore

Calcutta

3,3

Dacca

Tripura

Mizoram

December 1971
Indian support for
Bangladesh
guerrillas fighting for
independence
from Pakistan

Chittagong

1969 to Burma

● Mandalay

MYANMAR
from 1989
(BURMA)

Orissa

Bay of Bengal

Andaman Is.
to India

N

Moulmein

Bassein Rangoon

India: from decolonization
to nuclear rivalry

✳ unrest among tribal
minorities in Burma

✳ religious unrest and rivalry

Border wars

➤ Indian attacks

➤ Russian attacks

➤ Chinese attacks

➤ Pakistani attacks

Religious migrations
approximate numbers in millions

0,7 Muslims

0,7 Hindus

principalities were thereafter expected to adhere to either India or Pakistan, at the discretion of their rulers. This principle created difficulty in the state of Jammu and Kashmir, where a Hindu Maharaja ruled over a majority Muslim population. Within a month of independence, in August 1947, unrest among Kashmiri Muslims attracted intervention by what the UN would later describe as 'tribal forces' infiltrating from Pakistan. In October the Maharaja appealed to India for assistance, in exchange for which he was required to cast his lot with the government in New Delhi. Indian troops were then airlifted into Kashmir, and the matter brought to the attention of the United Nations. Pakistan denied complicity, then committed regular troops in May 1948. Fighting continued until the end of the year, when an uneasy UN ceasefire was brokered by the British generals who were still serving as chiefs of staff of the opposing armies. Muslim irregulars were left in control of about 5,000 square miles in Azad ('Free') Kashmir, in the northern part of the country. Its sovereignty is recognized by Pakistan, but no one else. The southern part, 80,000 square miles, became the Indian state of Jammu and Kashmir in 1963.

Border clashes remained endemic in Kashmir and elsewhere along the India–Pakistan frontier, notably in the Rann of Kutch, an almost uninhabitable salt marsh that became the scene of major fighting in 1965 and is still disputed territory. Of greater consequence was the conflict that arose in 1971, following a political crisis in Pakistan's remote eastern half. That Pakistan even had a remote eastern half was a reflection of the one-dimensional nature of the Islamic separatist movement to which the British had been compelled to accede in 1947. The area of Bengal that became East Pakistan was home to a Muslim population, but otherwise had no historical, linguistic, ethnic or economic connection to the main body of the Pakistani state, a thousand miles to the west. Politically under-represented and economically exploited, the people of East Pakistan came to feel that their status as a colony had not ended with the creation of the Pakistani state. This feeling was confirmed in 1970, when the first general election since independence returned a parliamentary

A postage stamp celebrates Bangladeshi statehood, 1971. Although East Pakistan won its independence because of Indian intervention, some 100,000 Bengalis took up arms during the war, so the image of the people triumphant is not entirely misplaced.

majority headed by an East Pakistani, Sheikh Mujibur Rahman. The military junta then ruling in Islamabad set the results aside and arrested Mujibur, who called for a general strike and demanded autonomy for his region.

War arose as a consequence of the murderous repression that this general strike brought down upon East Pakistan. By November 1971 as many as 6 million East Pakistanis had fled into India, pursued in some cases by elements of the Pakistani Army. Indian forces massed on the frontiers of both halves of Pakistan, though it was Pakistan that struck the first major blow, launching a pre-emptive air strike on the model of the Israeli operation that had destroyed the Egyptian Air Force a few years before. Its impact was negligible, as Pakistani intelligence failed to identify the location of India's planes, and because insufficient air assets were committed to it. Thereafter the initiative lay with the Indians, whose armoured forces moved rapidly into East Pakistan, surrounded on three sides by Indian territory. After a few days of hard fighting Pakistani resistance broke down under the converging Indian attacks, and because communications between East and West Pakistan, which traversed Indian territory and air space, were cut when India intervened.

Fighting also raged along the border with West Pakistan, though objectives there were mainly tactical. The partition of the Indian subcontinent had been conducted on the cusp of religious war. It had taken no account of natural terrain features, nor the need to create a frontier free of salients and exposed positions that invited border incursions. The crisis in East Pakistan created an opportunity to rectify this oversight. Each side committed about a dozen divisions to the task, which entailed hard fighting along the entire frontier. On the whole India did better, seizing almost 1,500 square miles of (mostly barren) Pakistani territory, while losing less than a hundred of its own. The border thereafter would remain roughly where the tanks stopped.

The 1971 war lasted a little over two weeks, reminiscent of contemporary conflicts in the Middle East, and equally reflective of the military superiority of one side. Indian casualties numbered around 7,000, of which about 1,500 were fatal. Pakistani casualties are unknown. Although dwarfed, in human terms, by the social violence of which it was merely an expression, the war was nevertheless a significant episode. East Pakistan became the independent republic of Bangladesh, a result that could not have been achieved without Indian intervention. The loss reduced Pakistan's standing in the region, and confirmed India's pre-eminence in South Asia.

Its broader effects were more ominous. India's military performance in 1971, far better than in its previous, more limited clashes with Pakistan, reflected the benefits of military assistance from the Soviet Union, to which India inclined, despite its formally non-aligned status. Pakistan enjoyed the less fulsome support of the United States, which sought at the last minute to lend a hand by dispatching an aircraft carrier carrying nuclear weapons into the Bay of Bengal, ostensibly to evacuate civilians, though it arrived too late to do so. India regarded this gesture as a threat, and embarked on its own nuclear programme the following year. Its first underground test was conducted in 1974, close enough to Pakistan for the vibrations to be felt by people in the street.

A similar combination of tribal and religious rivalries, and unresolved national aspirations, afflicted the new states of Africa, of which there were by 1980 approximately fifty, a number equal to the entire membership of the United Nations thirty-five years before. Although only a few of these achieved independence by war, most were nevertheless born in violent circumstances, or experienced internecine conflicts that sought to challenge or modify their presumptive national identities.

An example occurred in the British colony of Kenya. Kenya, like a number of African states, is named after its most prominent geographic feature – a mountain – rather than after any of the peoples who live there. Among these the most numerous were the Kikuyu. Like other tribal groups, the Kikuyu were confined to reservations during the colonial period in order to create land for white settlement, a condition they especially resented because it was their ancestral land, in what became known as the 'White Highlands', that proved most attractive to Europeans. As a new wave of European immigration began to rise after 1945, Kikuyu grievances crystallized within a secret society called the Mau Mau, which grew up inside Kenya's largest nationalist organization, the Kenya Africa Union (KAU). The Mau Mau organization mimicked that of leftist revolutionary groups around the world, with a cellular structure subdivided at the district and local levels, and a central committee in the capital. In reality, its outlook resembled that of the primitive rebels and machine breakers of earlier times. Members were bound to each other by elaborately ritualized blood oaths, and discipline was maintained by the personal fearsomeness of local leaders. At the height of their rebellion, only about 10 per cent had firearms. Attacks on Europeans were usually carried out simply to obtain them.

The Mau Mau embarked upon a campaign of terror in the autumn of 1952. Although nominally directed against whites, the vast majority of victims were other Kikuyu, eleven thousand of whom (along with ninety-five Europeans) died in gruesome fashion, literally at the hands of their tribal brethren. The suppression of the Mau Mau took four years – though the official state of emergency lasted until 1960, in order to extend the time arrested suspects could be kept in custody. At its height, the effort occupied 10,000 British soldiers, plus perhaps twice that many Kikuyu auxiliaries. It was the only major counter-insurgency campaign conducted by the British in Africa, and was carried out along lines similar to those employed with equal success in Malaya.

The relationship of the uprising to Kenyan nationalism is obscure. Shortly after Mau Mau attacks began, the British arrested the KAU leader, Jomo Kenyatta, and put him in jail for instigating the rebellion. Kenyatta, a Kikuyu himself, denied responsibility, a claim whose credibility is enhanced by his continued insistence upon it, even after Kenya achieved independence under his leadership in 1963. Still, it must be noted that the ceremony by which Mau Mau were inducted, which involved (among much else) butchering a goat, renouncing beer and cigarettes, and pledging support for female genital mutilation, concluded by invoking Kenyatta's name.

Kikuyu police auxiliaries armed with spears retire after searching a village for Mau Mau. Their prey were no better equipped.

To some extent the Mau Mau rebellion was a generational conflict. Many of the leaders were young men who had served in the British Army during the Second World War, while their victims were often tribal elders, whose acquiescence in British rule may have come to seem craven to those who had experienced a wider world. Whether the Mau Mau hastened Kenyan independence is hard to say. Certainly the social and political reforms carried out as part of the counter-insurgency campaign helped smooth the transfer of power later on. It also put paid to the notion that Kenya might become a white settler state like Southern Rhodesia, a thought in the minds of many of the whites who moved in after 1945; but this was not an idea that attracted the sympathy of the British government, which refused to involve the settlers in the suppression of the rebellion. There were no *pieds noirs* revolutionaries in Kenya, which is one reason the country survived its civil war intact.

In the final analysis, the distinctive feature of Kenya's war, apart from its intra-tribal nature, may simply be that it occurred before self-government was achieved, rather than afterwards. A contrasting, and more disastrous, case is afforded by the Belgian Congo, which dissolved in a flood of political violence immediately upon obtaining independence in 1960. Belgium had done next to nothing to prepare its colony for self-rule. Its departure was simply a reflection of its own inability to continue bearing the burdens of colonial stewardship. When the Belgians left, political authority was vested in a hastily conceived parliamentary government headed by Patrice Lumumba, the leading figure of the Congolese National Movement. He immediately faced dissention within Congo's security forces, which rebelled against the Belgian officers left behind to train them. Most Europeans remaining in the country fled. A month later the southernmost of the country's six major provinces, Katanga (Shaba), seceded. Lumumba appealed to the Soviet Union and to the UN for assistance. Both sent troops, though not in time to save Lumumba, who was overthrown in a coup and murdered by Katangan rebels.

AFRICA 1936 AND 1994

Until the 1880s Europeans knew little of Africa beyond the coastal regions and river deltas. Twenty years later, every inch was spoken for. Their departure after 1950 was equally precipitate, and no less problematic for the native peoples they had ruled.

Africa 1936

- ☐ Independent state with date
- ☐ British possession
- ☐ French possession
- ☐ Portuguese possession
- ☐ Spanish possession
- ☐ Italian possession
- ☐ Belgian possession

UN forces finally regained control in Katanga in January 1963, but the appearance that order had been restored was deceptive. When the last UN troops left in June 1964, secessionist violence erupted again, this time in the north and east, under the leadership of a vaguely leftist group called the Popular Army of Liberation, which enjoyed modest

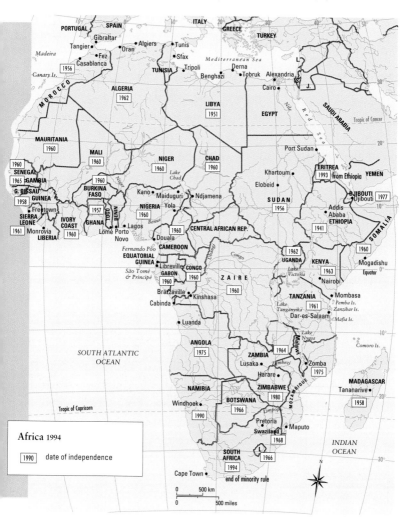

Africa 1994

1990   date of independence

end of minority rule

SOUTH ATLANTIC OCEAN

INDIAN OCEAN

0   500 km

0   500 miles

backing from the Soviet Union and China. In August the government, now headed by former Katangan separatist leader Moise Tsombe, called upon the United States and Belgium to intervene. Neither was prepared to do so on any scale, though in November 1964 they mounted a combined airborne operation (Belgian paratroops in American planes) to rescue 1,200 Europeans being held hostage by rebel forces in Stanleyville (Kisangani). This operation was co-ordinated with the Congolese Army, now led at the tactical level by white mercenaries recruited by Tsombe. It managed to use the success at Stanleyville to get its feet under itself, and over the next year a modicum of order was restored; whereupon the army's commander, Joseph Mobutu, overthrew the government, expelled the white mercenaries, and established an autocratic regime with himself at its head. He ruled the country, which he renamed Zaire, until he was himself ousted in a coup in 1997.

Katanga was a mineral-rich area, whose provincial identity was a creation of the colonial economy. Its separatist movement was driven by material motives, and was led by Africans linked to European mining interests there. Although it would be fair to describe much of the resulting violence that washed across the rest of the country as tribal in character, this was an exiguous feature: there are over two hundred tribal groups in the Congo (as the country is again known today), all but a few of which are too small to mount a significant rebellion.

A clearer case of ethnic war arose in Nigeria, Africa's most populous country, and the scene of one of its worst post-colonial uprisings. The British colony of Nigeria brought together four tribal groups, each of which is as large as the average African nation. Colonial administration had been based upon the principle of divide and rule, with a relatively weak central authority managing relations among strong regional governments. A similar system operated after Nigeria became independent in 1960. Sectional tension remained endemic. Over this was laid religious division, between Nigeria's Islamic north and west, and the Christian Igbo in the south-east. Religious difference led to diverging social and economic development, since, by resisting the activities of Christian missionaries, Nigeria's Muslims also cut themselves off from the benefits of western-style schooling.

When Nigeria became independent, the Igbo were, in material and educational terms, the most successful and enterprising of its peoples. Their position was further enhanced by the discovery of oil in the area where they predominated, which made independence a realistic possibility economically. Nevertheless, the Igbo sought to secede more from fear than ambition. More than most of their countrymen, the Igbo identified with the Nigerian state. They played a disproportionate role in its army and civil service, and their population was more widely distributed than that of the other tribal groups.

By 1966, the position of Nigeria's weak federal government had become untenable. A military regime took over, headed by an Igbo, Major General Johnson Aguiyi-Ironsi, who put forward a plan to replace Nigeria's regional governments with a strong central administration. His proposal was seen as a scheme to promote Igbo ascendancy, and sparked anti-Igbo rioting in which thousands died. Ironsi was assassinated by northern officers, and replaced as head of state by Lieutenant Colonel, later General, Yakubu Gowon, who convened a series of conferences to mediate intercommunal disputes. At the same time, Igbo from around the country streamed back towards the south-east, creating a refugee crisis of massive proportions. In May 1967, after efforts to arrive at a new constitutional settlement deadlocked, the governor of the Igbo region, Colonel Odumegwu Ojukwu, declared that his people faced genocide, and, acting on the instructions of the regional assembly, declared independence as the Republic of Biafra.

At first Biafran forces – which included half of Nigeria's trained officers – did well against their more numerous opponents, embarking upon offensive operations intended, like those of the Confederacy in the American Civil War, to shock their opponent into acquiescing to

WARS OF NATIONAL LIBERATION

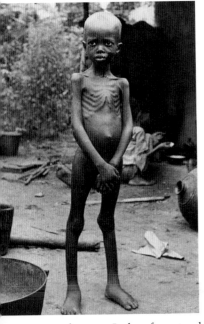

*A starving child in a Biafran refugee camp.
Such images defined the Nigerian civil war
in the eyes of the world, but did not inspire
international intervention to force a
settlement. On the contrary: the war lasted
as long as it did only because both sides
received assistance from abroad.*

secession. Their early advances sowed secessionist sentiment elsewhere, and there can be little question that, had Biafra won its independence, the rest of Nigeria would have disintegrated.

Both sides sought international assistance, with singular results. British companies owned important rights to the output of Biafra's oil fields. At the same time, its Labour government had no wish to revive colonial attachments. It therefore stood by its former colony out of loyalty, but declined to send anything other than small arms because it hoped to avoid escalation. France supported the rebels, to the point of providing them with surplus American war planes. It reasoned that the destruction of the largest anglophone state in Africa was in its interest. The United States did nothing. White Rhodesia sent arms to its fellow Christians in Biafra. The Soviet Union backed Nigeria's military government, apparently because British and American diffidence provided an opportunity to be on the winning side of an African war. It would be Soviet heavy weapons and military aircraft that would allow Gowon's junta to defeat Biafra's bid for national liberation.

Without international support, the Biafran war could not have lasted more than a few months. It actually lasted two and a half years. Given the means to hold out, the Igbo did so to the bitter end, being convinced that they would be slaughtered if they conceded defeat. The war's dominant note was therefore starvation, from which between 1 and 3 million Biafrans perished. This result was partly the accomplishment of the Nigerian Navy, a small fleet of patrol boats whose blockade line remained inviolate. Both sides suffered about 100,000 military casualties, a number exceeding the total strength of the Nigerian Army when the war began. Afterwards the Igbo were not slaughtered. Gowon proclaimed a general amnesty, declaring that there could be no blame and no victory in a war among brothers.

It remains to say a word about the African conflicts least likely to be mistaken for wars among brothers – those fought against the Portuguese by Africans in Guinea, Angola and Mozambique. Portugal was the only European country to fight hard to retain its position in sub-Saharan Africa. Its reasons for doing so resemble those that kept France in Algeria. Like France, Portugal imagined itself embarked upon a civilizing mission whose main beneficiaries would be the native peoples brought under its authority. After 1951 its African colonies were treated as overseas provinces, although only a small 'assimilated' fraction of the indigenous population was accorded rights of citizenship. Portugal's empire also appealed to the vanity of its proto-fascist government, headed by Antonio Salazar, who ruled as a dictator from 1933 until a stroke in 1968 which led his death two years later.

The wars Portugal faced were diffuse rural insurgencies, led by assimilated natives who had been exposed to Western education and Marxist ideas. Guinea and Mozambique produced relatively cohesive liberation fronts, partly tribal in character, but trained and armed by Eastern bloc countries and Algeria. In Angola, the revolutionary movement subdivided into three competing organizations: the Popular Movement for the Liberation of Angola (MPLA), based in the capital of Luanda; the Angolan National Liberation Front (FNLA), based on Angola's northern tribes; and the National Union for the Total Independence of Angola (UNITA), a splinter group from the FNLA that predominated in the south and east. The armed forces of all these groups numbered in the low thousands.

Serious fighting in all three countries arose in the early 1960s, and lasted until 1974, when a military coup put an end to Portuguese participation. Militarily, the guerrillas in Guinea had done best, establishing rural base areas comprising about 50 per cent of the country. Guerrilla groups in Angola and Mozambique rarely penetrated much beyond the border districts – all enjoyed sanctuary in neighbouring states – though in rural areas they could move freely over large areas, and offensive sweeps by Portuguese forces often failed to make contact with

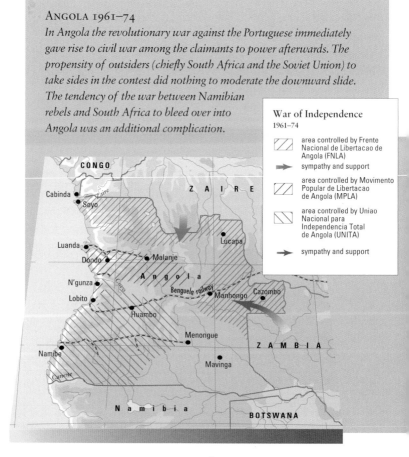

Angola 1961–74

In Angola the revolutionary war against the Portuguese immediately gave rise to civil war among the claimants to power afterwards. The propensity of outsiders (chiefly South Africa and the Soviet Union) to take sides in the contest did nothing to moderate the downward slide. The tendency of the war between Namibian rebels and South Africa to bleed over into Angola was an additional complication.

War of Independence
1961–74

area controlled by Frente Nacional de Libertacao de Angola (FNLA)

sympathy and support

area controlled by Movimento Popular de Libertacao de Angola (MPLA)

area controlled by Uniao Nacional para Independencia Total de Angola (UNITA)

sympathy and support

the enemy. Tactically, these were wars of ambushes and booby traps – 40 per cent of Portuguese casualties in Angola in 1970 were inflicted by mines – enlivened towards the end by long-range artillery and rocket fire, as the equipment of the insurgents improved. Portugal retained control of the cities in all three countries, and probably could have done so indefinitely, but at a cost far too great for it to bear. Portugal was and is the poorest country in Western Europe. At the climax of the struggle, it had about 150,000 troops in Africa, and 40 per cent of the national budget was devoted to defence. In proportional terms, both figures dwarf the American effort in Vietnam, and render implausible any claim that Portuguese conduct was motivated by economic or political rationality.

Afterwards, Guinea and Mozambique established one-party Marxist regimes, which sought to redress the inequities of colonialism by measures that were equally unpopular. Mozambique would find itself assailed in the 1970s by the anti-communist

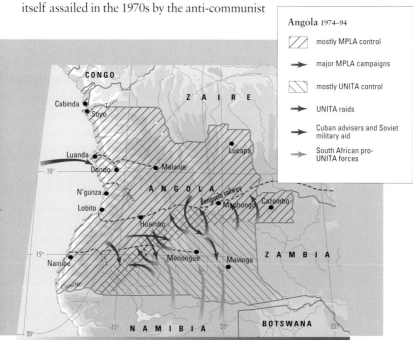

Angola 1974–94

╱╱ mostly MPLA control

→ major MPLA campaigns

╲╲ mostly UNITA control

➡ UNITA raids

➡ Cuban advisers and Soviet military aid

⇨ South African pro-UNITA forces

Mozambican National Resistance, a rural revolutionary group backed by Rhodesia. Worse awaited Angola, where the three revolutionary movements that fought the Portuguese fell upon each other. This provided new opportunities for outsiders. During the revolution, all of Angola's insurgents had been backed by the Soviet Union and its allies. Thereafter Soviet support gravitated towards the MPLA, which controlled the capital and became the recognized government. The FNLA and UNITA turned to the United States and South Africa. The United States sent money and weapons, funnelled through Zaire. South Africa intervened directly, partly with a view to establishing itself as the power broker in the region, partly to suppress a revolutionary group called SWAPO (South West Africa People's Organization), which operated against South Africa's Namibian protectorate from inside Angola. The Soviet Union responded by sponsoring an expeditionary force of 20,000 well-equipped Cuban troops.

The United States was not eager to see a direct confrontation between South Africa and a Soviet client, and South Africa soon withdrew its forces. Both the US and South Africa continued to support the FNLA and UNITA, however, and South African soldiers found their way back into Angola from time to time, though such incursions were denied or talked down. Serious fighting continued for fifteen years. The end of white rule in South Africa in 1989, and the collapse of the Soviet Union two years later, reduced the fuel by which the fire burned. It was only in 1997, however, that a tenuous government of national unity was achieved.

None of the contestants in Angola's civil war sought to alter the boundaries of the country. Whatever else they disagreed about, they accepted that Angola was a place whose geographical (and hence social) identity was settled. In this they were opposed throughout the 1970s by a little known fourth movement, called FLEC – Front for the Liberation of the Enclave of Cabinda. Cabinda is an oil patch north of the Zaire River, and is separated from the rest of Angola by a small neck of Congo territory at the river's mouth. Cabindan nationalism

A Portuguese weapons locker in Mozambique. All wars end, and always for a reason, but hardly ever because somebody runs out of ammunition.

received some backing from France, but has otherwise been deemed hopeless. This is because Cabinda is small – about 2,800 square miles – but also because secessionist movements directed against successor states have not enjoyed much sympathy among other Africans. This is evident, for instance, in the mediation efforts undertaken during the Biafran war by the Organization of African Unity, the quintessential expression of African nationalism as a general principle. Although the OAU, like the rest of the world, was appalled by the suffering in Biafra, it was not prepared to consider any solution that did not preserve a unified Nigerian state. In its view, national borders in Africa were sacrosanct.

To this day, most of those borders reflect the results of a conference held at Berlin in 1885, at which no Africans were present. There is an argument to be made that this imperial legacy is a disastrous burden, and more broadly that the idea of the nation state is irrelevant to African conditions – but, as the OAU's position on Biafra suggests, it is not an argument that has much standing in Africa itself. Few of its social and economic problems would be more easily addressed by governments made smaller and weaker by endlessly recursive subdivision. Those who have hoped that nationalism would introduce a theory of justice into international relations have been disappointed in Africa, as elsewhere. There is no morally convincing, theoretically grounded reason why Bangladesh should be a nation but not Biafra, Katanga, or even Cabinda. It is just that, in Africa especially, you have to draw the line somewhere.

CHAPTER SIX

Latin America

A young man and his trusty rocket-propelled grenade launcher. In this case the RPG is Soviet, the young man Salvadorean. Many other combinations were possible.

Latin America

In revolutionary war, any military action that needs explaining
to the people is politically useless.

Abraham Guillén, Strategy of the Urban Guerrilla

AT THE END of 1945 the United Nations had fifty members. Twenty were Central or South American republics, as compared to three from Africa and four from East Asia. Most had won their independence in the early nineteenth century, after the French Revolutionary and Napoleonic wars had loosened the grip of Spain and Portugal on their American colonies. The newest were Cuba, taken from Spain by the United States in 1898, and granted independence three years later; and Panama, which seceded from Colombia with American backing in 1903. The national liberation movements that swept across the region from the 1950s to the 1970s were thus not intended to create nation states, but to redress the social inequities that accompanied economic underdevelopment, and to throw off what some regarded as an illegitimate American hegemony.

Despite Latin America's political independence, there is no question that the regional economy resembled that of a colonial hinterland. Land was everywhere concentrated in few hands, manufacturing was rudimentary, population pressure severe. A disproportionate share of economic activity was devoted to producing agricultural goods and raw materials for export. As in the colonized world, the effect was to link the poorest segments of society to world markets for primary commodities, whose perturbations in the era of the world wars and the Great Depression became especially demoralizing. Economic and social instability provided fertile ground for oligarchic or dictatorial regimes, with which the United States co-operated, regardless of their methods or constitutional basis, because of its preponderant interest in maintaining order among its southern neighbours.

Since the promulgation of the Monroe Doctrine in 1823, the United States had regarded Latin America as its natural sphere of influence, from which European imperialism was excluded. This policy became more pronounced during the dramatic expansion of European empires towards the end of the nineteenth century. US opinion, preoccupied by the challenge of fulfilling the nation's 'manifest destiny' in North America, had always been reluctant to embrace the idea of overseas empire. Yet it also feared being disadvantaged by failing to do so. This ambivalence found expression in the Spanish–American War. While the rhetoric of 1898 was anti-imperialist, the reality was that the United States had gone to war not to vindicate Cuban independence, but from frustration over Spain's failure to crush Cuba's native liberation movement, and also from fear that Spain's weakness might

Fidel Castro in the Sierra Maestra, June 1957. Most of the leadership of Castro's movement is shown in this photograph. Che Guevara is second from the left. Raoul Castro, Fidel's younger brother, kneels with a rifle in the foreground. Two senior captains, Juan Almeida and George Sotus, stand to Castro's left and right. Far left is Lieutenant Universo Sanchez.

cause Cuba to fall into the hands of a stronger European power. Similar motives operated in Panama, whose independence was promoted to ensure that control of the long-planned Isthmian Canal would be in American hands.

These events marked less a change than a hardening of the United States' view of its interests to the south. They signalled the start of a pattern of military interventionism that lasted over thirty years, and involved dozens of expeditionary operations in the Caribbean and Central America. Although this militarized approach was abandoned during the Roosevelt administration, the enormous weight of US commercial interests in the region nevertheless created conditions that some observers found indistinguishable from colonial subjugation. This point of view was strengthened in the 1950s, when the US resumed an interventionist policy in order to forestall the spread of communism. Its chief instrument would be the Central Intelligence Agency. In 1954, the CIA organized the overthrow of a civilian and reformist government in Guatemala, the first in Latin America with communist participation, after its president, Jacobo Arbenz, attempted to nationalize some holdings of the United Fruit Company there – the first

LATIN AMERICA 1945–95

Few Latin American states proved immune to political violence of one form or another in the 1960s and 70s. Most survived their time of troubles to forge democratic regimes, a development that would have surprised many observers at the time, who imagined that a propensity for chaos had somehow been woven into the cultural fabric of the continent.

Ideological conflicts and revolutions
Political changes

■ social revolution
■ reformism
▪ populism
■ Christian democracy
■ unreformed militarism
■ guerrilla movements
□ establishing or re-establishing democratic rule
⚔ Cuban-inspired guerrilla movements 1959–68
➜ US intervention 1965–94

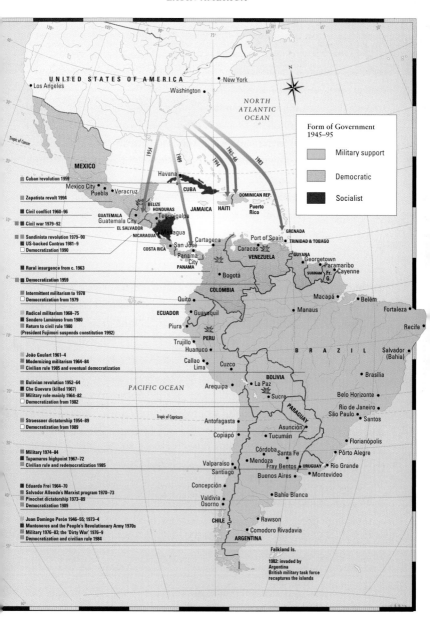

Form of Government
1945–95

Military support

Democratic

Socialist

UNITED STATES OF AMERICA
• Los Angeles
• New York
Washington •

NORTH
ATLANTIC
OCEAN

Tropic of Cancer

MEXICO
Cuban revolution 1959
Mexico City •
Puebla • Veracruz
Zapatista revolt 1994
Havana
CUBA
DOMINICAN REP.
BELIZE
HONDURAS
Civil conflict 1960–96
JAMAICA
HAITI
Puerto
Rico
Civil war 1979–92
GUATEMALA
Guatemala City
EL SALVADOR
Tegucigalpa
Sandinista revolution 1979–90
US-backed Contras 1981–9
Democratization 1990
NICARAGUA
Managua
COSTA RICA
• San José
Cartagena
GRENADA
Port of Spain • TRINIDAD & TOBAGO
Rural insurgence from c. 1963
Panama
City
PANAMA
Caracas
VENEZUELA
GUYANA
Georgetown
Paramaribo
SURINAM Fr. Cayenne
G.
Democratization 1959
• Bogotá
COLOMBIA
Intermittent militarism to 1978
Democratization from 1979
Quito •
ECUADOR
Guayaquil •
Macapá
Manaus
• Belém
Fortaleza •
Radical militarism 1968–75
Sendero Luminoso from 1980
Return to civil rule 1980
(President Fujimori suspends constitution 1992)
Piura •
Recife •
PERU
Trujillo •
Huanuco •
B R A Z I L
Salvador •
(Bahia)
João Goulart 1961–4
Modernizing militarism 1964–84
Civilian rule 1985 and eventual democratization
Callao •
Lima •
Cuzco •
BOLIVIA
• Brasília
Bolivian revolution 1952–64
Che Guevara (killed 1967)
Military rule mainly 1964–82
Democratization from 1982
PACIFIC OCEAN
Arequipa •
• La Paz
• Sucre
Belo Horizonte •
Rio de Janeiro •
São Paulo • • Santos
Stroessner dictatorship 1954–89
Democratization from 1989
Tropic of Capricorn
Antofagasta •
PARAGUAY
Asunción •
• Florianópolis
Military 1974–84
Tupamaros highpoint 1967–72
Civilian rule and redemocratization 1985
Copiapó •
Córdoba •
Santa Fe •
• Tucumán
• Pôrto Alegre
Eduardo Frei 1964–70
Salvador Allende's Marxist program 1970–73
Pinochet dictatorship 1973–89
Democratization 1989
Valparaíso •
Mendoza •
Fray Bentos • URUGUAY • Rio Grande
Santiago •
Buenos Aires •
• Montevideo
Juan Domingo Perón 1946–55; 1973–4
Montoneros and the People's Revolutionary Army 1970s
Military 1976–83; the 'Dirty War' 1976–9
Democratization and civilian rule 1984
Concepción •
Valdivia •
Osorno •
• Bahía Blanca
CHILE
• Rawson
• Comodoro Rivadavia
ARGENTINA

Falkland Is.

1982: invaded by
Argentina
British military task force
recaptures the islands

1954
1989
1994
1965–6
1963

clear indication that Latin America was destined to become at least a secondary theatre in the conduct of the Cold War. Yet the self-representation of Latin American revolutionaries as fighters against a foreign tyranny was never entirely successful. As in Africa, the real struggle lay within national communities in which other well-organized political forces were also present. It is for this reason that so few Latin American national liberation movements succeeded.

The onset of serious revolutionary activity dates from the triumph of Fidel Castro's guerrillas in 1959. Although the Cuban Revolution is remembered as a peasants' war, such an interpretation fails to capture the *sui generis* nature of Castro's success. Castro first tried to overthrow the Cuban government in 1953, by storming an army barracks outside Santiago with about two hundred men, in the hope of sparking a popular uprising. Most of the attackers were killed. Castro, sentenced to fifteen years in prison, was released under a general amnesty after eleven months, and went into exile in Mexico. He returned in December 1956, landing with eighty-one men on a remote stretch of Cuba's southern coast. The landing had been anticipated, however, and only a dozen of Castro's followers avoided death or capture. With these he escaped into the Sierra Maestra, where he set about building up his forces and harassing the authorities. Most early attacks were against private property, so as to avoid contact with security forces. Later engagements featured ambushes or assaults on rural police stations and army barracks. By the middle of 1958, Castro's forces were able to move more or less freely among the rural communities of Cuba's easternmost province, Oriente. Yet even at the end, he never had as many as a thousand men under arms.

Although the public jubilation that greeted Castro's entry into Havana was undoubtedly authentic, no violent mass uprising occurred. None was necessary. Since 1952, Cuba's government had been in the hands of Fulgencio Batista, a once-vigorous figure now in his dotage, whose personal rule exemplified sloth and corruption. These qualities permeated the army on which his regime depended. Cuban armed forces were untrained in counter-insurgency operations, and unmotivated to carry them out – in the entire course of the Cuban Revolution, only two hundred soldiers (out of 40,000) were killed. This defensive attitude was fatal against even a small band of highly motivated opponents. Rather than seek out the enemy, Cuban security forces responded to Castro's provocations with indiscriminate repression against all critics of the regime, which gradually united them behind Castro's visible and dynamic leadership. Once it became clear that Batista's government was unable to face down even so minor a threat as Castro's movement, middle-class opinion deserted it, having long since grown weary of the venality that was stifling economic growth. By the time Batista fled the country, even the clergy had turned against him.

Apart from the incompetence of his opponents, Castro's victory was aided by widespread uncertainty as to his intentions. Although he would later claim that his communist sympathies were well developed before the revolution, they were not apparent at the time. Had they been, it is unlikely that Cuban opinion would have rallied so readily to his cause, which most identified with clean and democratic government, land reform and social progress generally. Nor, one imagines, would the United States have confined itself, as it did, to imposing an arms embargo on the island, a measure that hurt Batista more than Castro.

Nevertheless, there was never any question that serious reform would transgress American interests. Foreigners, mostly Americans, owned 75 per cent of the arable land in Cuba, at a time when the average rural worker earned less than $100 per year. Castro nationalized those holdings, whereupon the US banned the importation of Cuban goods, for which it was the main overseas market. This measure hastened (if it did not cause) Castro's public identification with the Soviet bloc. The confiscation of private property also inspired an exodus of middle-class Cubans, who became vocal critics of the new regime. In May 1960 the CIA began providing clandestine training and support to Cuban exiles, with a view to retaking the island by force. This effort misfired at the Bay of Pigs in April 1961, and most of the 1,400-man invasion force was captured and held for ransom (eventually paid by private subscription). American efforts to isolate Cuba would thereafter remain unremitting, while Castro's government would become the principal exporter of communist revolution in the Western Hemisphere.

Castro's victory became the inspiration and model for a wave of rural insurgencies in Latin America in the 1960s, including major episodes in Brazil, Argentina, Venezuela, Peru, Colombia, Guatemala, Bolivia, and Nicaragua. All failed, though the Sandinistas of Nicaragua would eventually provide the leadership for the more broadly based movement that seized power in Managua in 1979. Although circumstances varied from one country to the next, the pervasive nature of the revolutionaries' defeat suggests that general factors were also at work.

One was simply the fact of Castro's success, which put all other governments in the region on alert. Cuba's new government drove home the lesson by trumpeting its determination to spread communism. No subsequent revolutionary group would be the beneficiary of the kind of uncritical bourgeois acquiescence that helped propel Castro's men into Havana. Castro made counter-insurgency the primary mission of Latin American armies. Many became quite proficient – a transformation aided by American money, training and equipment – and none exhibited anything like the ineptitude of Batista's forces. Methods tended to be harsh and directly military. Torture, paramilitary death squads, summary executions, systematic defoliation and reprisal terrorism were all part of the counter-revolutionary repertoire in Latin America. The US sought to link such measures to a variety of social palliatives under a policy known as the Alliance for Progress, but its effects were hampered by the reluctance of Latin American élites to tolerate any intrusion upon issues of land tenure, and also by the disinclination of Latin American armies to involve themselves in manual labour and non-military public works programmes. Although it is commonly believed that bad governments cannot save themselves by repression alone, the Latin American experience in the 1960s and 70s offers ample evidence to the contrary.

Latin American revolutionaries failed to grasp the improbability of the Cuban example, which was supposed to exemplify the nation in arms, but was in reality something closer to Mussolini's March on Rome. The evangelist of Castro's revolution was one of his lieutenants, Ernesto 'Che' Guevara, whose book *Guerrilla Warfare* (1959) appeared on the eve of victory, and immediately acquired enormous cachet. Guevara was a man of action. His theoretical principles were few in number and basically simple, which no doubt heightened their appeal. They were:

1) Popular forces can win a war against the army.

2) It is not necessary to wait until all conditions for making revolution exist; the insurrection can create them.

3) In underdeveloped America the countryside is the basic area for armed fighting.

All three of these propositions stood at some remove from classic communist theorizing about revolutionary war. The first is true enough, but within limits that had already been apparent to Marx and Engels, who doubted that a government backed by a modern army of even moderate competence could be overthrown by force. It was for this reason that revolutionary violence had to await the maturation of favourable social conditions. Even then, its use required careful preparation under the leadership of a revolutionary party. Lenin and Mao had elaborated upon this thought, placing greater weight on the decisiveness of force – political power growing from the barrel of a gun, as Mao said – while continuing to affirm the primacy of politics. Mao especially had envisioned the revolutionary climacteric in military terms: victory would come when the party disposed of regular forces capable of defeating those of the state.

A billboard face painting of Che Guevara. Che imagined himself revolutionizing a continent, and died in the attempt.

Guevara, on the other hand, rejected the idea that revolutionary success depended upon favourable social conditions, or even upon the guidance of a revolutionary party. His first principle must be understood in the light of the second: that it is insurrection that creates revolutionary conditions, and not the other way around. The distinctive feature of Latin American revolutionary doctrine was the proposition that violence can transform the political environment in ways that make a protracted period of political organization and social mobilization unnecessary. Régis Debray, one of Guevara's compatriots, dubbed this approach *foquismo*, after the small guerrilla band, or *foco* ('centre'), whose bold actions would inspire the people by demonstrating that resistance was possible.

Foquismo was justified by reference to local conditions, particularly the difficulty of defending territorial bases in relatively small, highly militarized countries. Its deepest roots, however, were not tactical, but moral. Guevara, Debray and their contemporaries have much to say about courage, honour and vengeance; about sacrifice and the importance of hating the enemy. In their eyes, revolutionary violence was not part of some complex dialectic. It was a heroic gesture, propaganda by deed – closer to anarchism or fascism than to mainstream Marxism, which was all about patience and timing. In practice, *foquismo* often became *golpismo* – the belief that success would come from one powerful push (*golpe*). Early setbacks, which guerrilla movements must normally take for granted, could thus have disproportionate, sometimes decisive, effects.

In Guevara's analysis, the obstacles to revolution in Latin America were psychological. It was thus of particular importance that the scene of revolutionary struggle was supposed to be the countryside. Latin American peasants possess all the scepticism for which their counterparts are known around the world, and proved highly resistant to the semiotics of *foquismo*. They stood ready to defend their land, and seize the property of the local grandee if the opportunity arose. But they were inconstant allies in adversity, and were inclined to betray guerrillas who could not keep the authorities away. The mobile *foci*, unable to secure permanent bases for themselves, were also poor vehicles for recruitment. Even peasants willing to take up arms against the regime were rarely willing to leave their native areas to do so. Finally, in Latin America as throughout the world, the revolutionary leadership consisted almost exclusively of young, well-educated men from relatively prosperous, cosmopolitan backgrounds. The cultural distance separating them from the rural peasantry could only be bridged by prolonged and constructive acquaintance of the kind that *foquismo* ruled out.

By the late 1960s rural insurgency on the Guevarist model had been largely defeated in Latin America – the symbolic climax came in 1967, when Guevara himself was killed fighting in Bolivia. Thereafter the centre of conflict shifted to the cities. In a few cases it had always been there. Communist revolutionaries in the early sixties came closest to victory in one of Latin America's most democratic countries, Venezuela. Its National Liberation Armed Forces (FALN), openly supported by Cuba, had always been based in Caracas, which became the scene of intense fighting in 1962–3. The FALN experience was in many respects typical. Early attacks upon police – the goal was to kill one per day – were unsettling to public opinion, and put pressure on the regime to take potentially delegitimizing action to defend itself. As the violence escalated to include targets like banks and trains, however, public disaffection turned against the rebels, who then became subject to brutal counter-measures.

It was also characteristic that the FALN did not dissolve in defeat, but splintered instead. Factionalism was endemic in most Latin American revolutionary movements, always with debilitating results. Most FALN cadres accepted the public amnesty offered by the government in 1964. Some would go on to serve in the Venezuelan Congress. Others, however, reverted to rural insurrection, under the leadership of the redoubtable Douglas Bravo, who set a standard for personal determination that few of his contemporaries would match. Bravo and his men were driven so far on to the margins of Venezuelan society that fewer than a dozen were killed by the authorities in all of the 1970s. Yet it was only in 1979 that he finally laid down his arms.

The rise of the urban guerrilla was driven by the logic of *foquismo*. Cities provided a more hospitable social environment for the revolutionaries themselves, but mainly they ensured that the revolutionaries' deeds would be visible, a requirement if they were to achieve the desired impact. The Brazilian Carlos Marighela, whose *Handbook of Urban Guerrilla Warfare* became almost as famous as Che's work, compared publicity to a gun lying in the street, free for anyone to use. Yet working on a brighter stage could present problems. Abraham Guillén, whose ideas helped inspire the Tupamaros of Uruguay, complained, for instance, that the practice of kidnapping public officials and holding them for monetary ransom – a Tupamaros speciality – made them indistinguishable from a crime syndicate in the eyes of the people; while killing the hostage after making a show of capturing him made martyrs of the victim's wife and children.

Despite such tactical difficulties, the Tupamaros would become the most celebrated of Latin America's urban guerrilla movements, in part because, like Venezuela's FALN, they had the advantage of operating in a democratic country. Uruguay was far slower to adopt ruthless measures than its neighbours, Brazil and Argentina, who experienced similar problems. From 1968 to 1972 Tupamaros waged an artfully conceived campaign of provocation, less indiscriminately violent than most, and well-calculated to humiliate the regime. Kidnapping was prominent within the Tupamaros repertoire because, even if the public

The crumbled remains of the Bowling Club in Montevideo, Uruguay, demolished by a Tupamaros bomb in September 1970. The Tupamaros consistently targeted the lives and property of the rich, a by no means universal practice, since it is usually the poor who lack police protection. The brazenness of such attacks was part of the message.

could be persuaded that the government could not save people from being killed at random, most still thought the authorities ought to be able to save captives being held alive in 'prisons of the people'. For over three years no Tupamaros' hostage was ever rescued by the police, a record of futility that, in a period of economic turmoil and hyper-inflation, did much to undermine the regime. In 1972, however, the army took over, after which the Tupamaros were wrapped up in short order. Régis Debray would write later on that the Tupamaros dug the grave of democracy in Uruguay, and then fell in.

The same cannot be said for the one Latin American leftist movement, apart from Castro's, to seize power for itself. The Sandinista National Liberation Front (FSLN) in Nicaragua originated as a Guevarist insurgency in 1961. By 1967, the movement had been reduced to the status of a secret society for students and trade unionists, in which form it would survive until a combination of constitutional crisis and natural disaster provided a signal for renewed action. Nicaragua was then governed by Anastasio Somoza, whose family had ruled the country since 1937. In 1972, a constitutional nicety made it impossible for Somoza to succeed himself as president. He therefore created a puppet cabinet with himself holding the strings as commander of the National Guard, long the basis of his family's power. This ramshackle regime collapsed because of its failure to provide relief following the massive earthquake that struck Managua in December, a catastrophe from which Somoza profited in conspicuous fashion, by diverting international aid, and also by exploiting the desperation of the population. One such venture involved buying blood from displaced persons for a few pennies, and then exporting it to commercial blood banks in the US. Afterwards Somoza redrew the constitution to allow him to resume the presidency.

These events brought political opposition back to the surface of Nicaraguan society, initially under the leadership of the Democratic Union of Liberation (UDEL), headed by Pedro Chamorro. In time, however, the Sandinistas would prove the more dynamic organization.

Nicaraguan soldiers resting alongside a wall painting of Augusto Sandino (1893–1934), namesake of the Sandinistas. Sandino led the resistance to US intervention in Nicaragua from 1927 to 1934. After he came out of hiding he was assassinated by National Guard officers under Anastasio Somoza García, father of the man the Sandinistas would overthrow.

In 1974, they staged a brilliant kidnapping of dozens of Somoza confederates, and obtained money and political concessions in return for their release. The government responded with an indiscriminate counter-insurgency campaign, often against villages in remote regions the Sandinistas had long since abandoned. Thousands died, including one of the Sandinista's founders, Carlos Fonseca; also Chamorro, who was assassinated for exposing Somoza's blood bank scheme in January 1978. His death sparked a general strike lasting two weeks, in which participation was by no means confined to the workers. Thereafter, popular unrest was rarely absent from the cities of Nicaragua. The FSLN, which inherited the mantle of revolutionary leadership following the death of Chamorro, did its part to stimulate insurrection

A subdued band of Sandinistas pose with a light machine-gun. One fellow at the back tries for a more enthusiastic tone.

by bold actions – this was *foquismo* indeed, but in a context where daring deeds would echo throughout society.

Like Castro, the Sandinistas succeeded because they rode a wave of general discontent that transcended the social divisions the regime had exploited to maintain itself. In contrast to the Cuban case, however, the revolution in Nicaragua was hard fought. Some 30,000 died, and another 500,000 were left homeless, an enormous burden in an already impoverished country of 4 million people. Nothing in the Sandinistas' conventionally leftist programme of economic nationalization was useful in these circumstances. Such measures offended middle-class groups and the Church, and alarmed the US, which had played the role of ineffectual mediator during the civil war, and now set about trying to overthrow the new regime. US aid to Nicaragua ended following the inauguration of Ronald Reagan as President in 1981. Shortly thereafter the Sandinistas called off a planned election, after which defections from their movement increased. Some of these found their way into the Contras, a counter-revolutionary guerrilla force based in Honduras, which was sustained by US money and arms. Nicaragua responded by serving as a conduit for Soviet aid to communist rebels in El Salvador. An election that was deemed fair by international observers was held in 1984, and produced a clear Sandinista victory, but did not end American military and economic pressure. Although direct support for the Contras was cut off in 1987, a US trade embargo remained in place until 1990, when a new election brought Pedro Chamorro's widow, Violeta, to power.

National liberation movements in Latin America proved to be obstacles to democracy and social progress. They kept alive habits of personal and military rule, and discredited voices of liberal reform that always existed, but could scarcely make themselves heard above the rattle of gunfire. The military governments that arose to confront the revolutionary emergencies of the 1960s and 70s were ill-equipped to cope with the prolonged world recession of the 1980s, and most would accordingly be replaced by more economically literate civilian regimes. A partial exception may be made for the Sandinistas, the only revolutionary movement in the region that can plausibly be said to have advanced the cause of responsible government, however imperfectly they may have embodied it themselves. The best testimony to the authenticity of their revolutionary credentials was their willingness to accept defeat in an election. Within the framework of Latin American politics since the 1960s, few bolder gestures were possible. Afterwards they continued to exist as a legal opposition party within a democratic state – not where they expected to be, but better than where they began, and better than anything they could have expected from the regime they helped overthrow.

CHAPTER SEVEN

Israel

*A boatload of Jewish refugees, stopped for
inspection in the Bay of Haifa, August 1946.
When caught, refugees were sent to Cyprus for
processing, and then back to Europe. Most,
having lost everything already, would simply
try again.*

Israel

Thou land devourest up men, and hast bereaved thy nations.

Ezekiel 36:13

THE WARS THAT created the state of Israel, and may yet create the state of Palestine, are rooted in the migration of European Jews to the Levant beginning in the 1880s, and in the reactions this movement inspired within the international community, and among the Arabs. Zionism, in the eyes of its founder, Theodor Herzl, was a national and not an imperial cause, intended to restore a community broken by historical accident. The Jews did not go to Palestine as conquerors, but as immigrants in search of a better life, and as refugees from persecution. Jews settled on land purchased from Arab and Turkish landlords, or reclaimed marshes and wasteland for farming and commerce. Their arrival inspired resistance from the start, though intercommunal violence against Jews before 1914 was not categorically different from that suffered by Armenians, Assyrians, Kurds, Balkan Christians, and other minorities within the Ottoman Empire.

When the empire's future was cast into final jeopardy by its entry into the First World War, rivalries among the groups who hoped to found successor regimes intensified. The British fomented rebellion by the Arabs against the Turks, and promised to support their independence. They also appealed to international Zionism, which was thought to be influential in Russia and the United States, and endorsed the establishment in Palestine of a Jewish 'national home'. Both pledges were crafted to provide room for manoeuvre. In their dealings with the Arabs, the British excluded Palestine from the territory of a prospective Arab state. Support for a Jewish homeland was likewise contingent on nothing being done to prejudice the rights of non-Jews.

After the war these promises were neither fulfilled nor reconciled, the latter being, perhaps, impossible. Arab aspirations were subordinated to a system of League mandates that appeared little different from a new imperial regime. The knowledge that the British intended to convey at least part of the Palestine Mandate to the Jews was an additional grievance. The Arabs did not understand how land they had occupied for centuries could be taken away so capriciously. The British believed they had created the conditions for Arab statehood by defeating the Ottomans, and should be allowed some discretion in disposing of the fruits of that victory. The Jews were less unhappy than the Arabs, since postponing a decision favoured them: Jews constituted only about 10 per cent of the population of Palestine when the First World War ended. The early Zionists, moreover, had always imagined that the Jewish State would be created by international agreement and conciliation. Thus the Yishuv, as the Jewish community in Palestine was called, was prepared to wait upon the workings of the League.

The prospect that the imbalance between Jews and Arabs might be altered by further Jewish settlement alarmed Arab leaders, and anti-

Jewish settlers in Palestine erecting a barbed-wire fence to protect themselves from Arab attacks, October 1938. The tall objects are iron fence posts.

Jewish violence increased along with Jewish numbers throughout the 1920s. Hitler's rise to power forced a crisis. Jewish immigration accelerated, while Britain became anxious that allowing it might alienate the Arabs, whose support would be important in any future war with Germany. A crossover point was reached in 1936, when a general strike incited by the Mufti of Jerusalem led to ferocious violence against Jews that persisted for months. Afterwards Britain took steps to limit Jewish immigration, a grievous policy it felt compelled to adopt given the depth of Arab resentment, to which must be added that of millions of non-Arab Muslims who were then subjects of the British Empire. The British decision to restrict Jewish settlement to a level acceptable to the Arabs eliminated any hope that Jewish statehood could be achieved peacefully. Nevertheless, the Zionists had no choice but to support Britain against the Nazis. It was only after Germany's defeat was certain that serious conflict between Britain and the Yishuv became possible.

The Yishuv included within it a number of armed groups. The most important was the Hagana, the semi-secret military arm of the Jewish Agency, which co-ordinated immigration, and helped manage Jewish affairs in the Mandate. Hagana's ethos was defensive – it had been created to protect Jewish settlements against Arab attacks – but it acquired striking power during the war, when special units of shock troops (Palmach) were trained by the British to repel Axis forces that might appear in the region. Alongside the Hagana was the IZL (Irgun Zvai Leumi, or National Military Organization), an underground organization founded by Hagana dissidents and led, after 1943, by Menachem Begin. The IZL believed a Jewish state could only be founded by force, and when Whitehall's policy shifted towards the Arabs it turned against the British. The IZL later produced an even more extreme faction, the LHI (Lohamey Heruth Israel, or Fighters for the Freedom of Israel), known after its founder as the Stern gang. Anti-British terrorism by the IZL and LHI moderated during the war, in part because it was suppressed by the Hagana. Afterwards, when the British declined to reverse their strictures on immigration, all three became uneasy allies in a campaign to drive the British out.

From the autumn of 1945, Palestine became the scene, for the first time, of widespread violence instigated by Jews. Most attacks took the form of bomb attacks on public infrastructure, though the IZL and the Stern gang did not shrink from the deliberate killing of British soldiers and police. The British came to regard the entire Jewish population as hostile, and imposed something approaching military rule. A climax was reached in the summer of 1946, when the Irgun blew up the wing of the King David Hotel in Jerusalem that housed British police headquarters, an act that shocked world opinion. So, too, did the recurring spectacle of British soldiers manhandling penurious Jewish refugees, most of whom had just escaped death at the hands of the Nazis.

At the start of 1947, Britain had 100,000 troops in Palestine. The question why had to be faced. Before the Arab uprising in 1936, British policy aimed at the creation of a single Palestinian state in which Jews and Arabs would rule together. Afterwards thoughts turned to partition, an approach grudgingly accepted by the Zionists but not by the Arabs. A number of schemes were produced by Whitehall and the Jewish Agency before the war. As Britain grew weary of its Mandatory burden, this process revived under the auspices of a United Nations committee. Its report was adopted by the General Assembly in November 1947, and called for a Jewish state in three barely contiguous parts, with Jerusalem as an international city. The UN vote was a deliverance

A soldier of the Hagana, identified by the brand on his arm as death camp inmate 80620, standing guard in Jaffa. The impact of such images, and of the unique moral context to which they testified, can scarcely be overestimated.

for the British, but it was an expression of US policy. American opinion had been revolted by the revelation of the Holocaust in Europe, and the Truman administration was unwilling to face the political consequences that would follow a further affront to America's strongly Zionist Jewish community. Politics in any case is about choices, and by 1948 there were no good ones left in Palestine.

With the announcement of the UN plan, fighting between Jews and Arabs resumed in earnest, as both sides sought to improve their position in preparation for the showdown to come. Israel declared independence on the day the last British troops left, on 14 May 1948. The next day the armies of five Arab states attacked. The odds of Israel's survival were long, but not as desperate as they might have appeared. Israeli forces, although outnumbered, were better trained than their opponents, and fought under a unified command, an important achievement that required the forcible subordination of the IZL and the LHI to the Hagana, now rechristened the Israeli Defence Force (IDF). Neither side possessed much in the way of heavy weapons, which meant that Israeli tactical proficiency counted for even more than it otherwise might have. All combatants laboured under an international arms embargo organized by the US, which the Israelis were more successful at circumventing, having prepared for it in advance. The Jews also fought on 'interior lines', while the logistics of Arab armies, especially those of Egypt and Iraq, were attenuated and vulnerable to attack.

THE WAR OF ISRAELI INDEPENDENCE 1948–9

Israel's victory in 1948 was a product of superior military organization, superior social cohesion and a well-developed network of support from Jews overseas. Their money made timely arms purchases possible, without which the war might have been lost. As it was, Jewish casualties were heavier than in any of Israel's later wars, amounting to almost six thousand dead – in relative terms, a toll comparable to Britain's in the First World War.

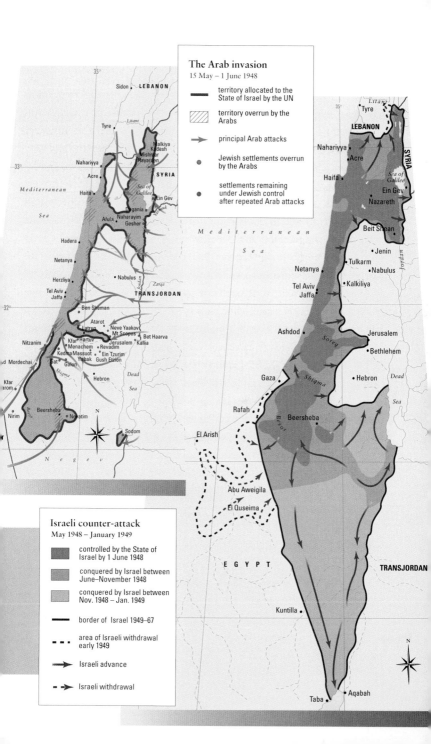

The Arab invasion
15 May – 1 June 1948

- territory allocated to the State of Israel by the UN
- territory overrun by the Arabs
- principal Arab attacks
- Jewish settlements overrun by the Arabs
- settlements remaining under Jewish control after repeated Arab attacks

Israeli counter-attack
May 1948 – January 1949

- controlled by the State of Israel by 1 June 1948
- conquered by Israel between June–November 1948
- conquered by Israel between Nov. 1948 – Jan. 1949
- border of Israel 1949–67
- area of Israeli withdrawal early 1949
- Israeli advance
- Israeli withdrawal

Left map labels:

LEBANON
Sidon
Tyre
Litani
Nahariyya
Malkiya
Kedesh
Mishmar Hayarden
Acre
SYRIA
Haita
Sea of Galilee
Ein Gev
Dagania
Afula
Naharayim Gesher
Yarmuk
Mediterranean Sea
Hadera
Netanya
Herzliya
Nabulus
Zaqa
Tel Aviv
Jaffa
TRANSJORDAN
Jordan
Ben Sheman
Atarot
Latrun
Neve Yaakov
Mt Scopus
Bet Haarva
Nitzanim
Kfar Hartuv
Menachem
Revadim
Jerusalem
Kalia
Kedma
Massuot
Ein Tzurim
Yibhak
Gush Etzion
Gat
Galon
Mordechai
Shiqma
Hebron
Dead Sea
Kfar arom
Besor
Beersheba
Nevatim
Nirim
Sodom
N e g e v
Sodom
N

Right map labels:

Litani
Tyre
LEBANON
SYRIA
Nahariyya
Acre
Sea of Galilee
Haifa
Ein Gev
Nazareth
Beit Shean
Jenin
Mediterranean Sea
Netanya
Tulkarm
Nabulus
Tel Aviv
Kalkiliya
Jaffa
Ashdod
Soreq
Jerusalem
Bethlehem
Gaza
Shiqma
Hebron
Dead Sea
Rafah
Besor
Beersheba
El Arish
Abu Aweigila
El Quseima
E G Y P T
TRANSJORDAN
Kuntilla
N
Taba
Aqabah

Arab forces, comprised overwhelmingly of peasant conscripts, were tenacious in defence, but showed little capacity for independent action, and had difficulty manoeuvring when in contact with the enemy. This was not a reflection upon their personal courage, but upon the low level of social cohesion that prevailed within the autocratic, semi-feudal regimes for which they fought – conditions from which Western-style armies like the IDF have benefited around the world. Finally, Israel's assailants had no common strategy, and squabbled among themselves. They also underestimated their enemy. The Arabs proclaimed a holy war, but it was the Jews, with nowhere to run, who fought one.

The War of Israeli Independence culminated in a series of bilateral ceasefires in 1949. It would be thirty years before any Arab state was prepared to accept the outcome as final, for reasons that were to some extent apparent on a map. Although Israeli forces had seized territory beyond what was allotted to the Jews by the UN, the result was still a state with barely defensible frontiers and no strategic depth. When the fighting stopped, most Israelis still lived within range of someone else's artillery. The war also created 700,000 Palestinian refugees, whose presence became a burden and a reproach to Israel's foes. Most Palestinians would be consigned by their hosts to nominally temporary camps, there to await Israel's eradication. These became bases for terrorism, and forcing beds for Palestinian national identity. Although 160,000 Arabs became citizens of Israel after the war, those who left were not allowed to return in the absence of a general settlement. Their places were eventually taken by half a million Jews, fleeing Arab lands where they had once resided in peace.

Israeli strategy would be dominated by these geographic and social facts. Terrorism and harassing bombardments became facts of life, and were met by reprisals and counter-terrorism. Although it was possible that such clashes might escalate into something larger, they did not threaten the new state's existence in themselves. Real danger lay in the prospect of conventional defeat. Disaster was most likely to result from being taken by surprise at the outset of a new war. If, as Clausewitz said, the essence of the defensive is awaiting the blow, this was an attitude denied to the Israelis, who could not retreat in order to trade space for time. Nor could Israel afford protracted conflict. Its defence required the mobilization of large civilian reserves, who could not be withdrawn from the economy indefinitely. IDF doctrine evolved to meet these requirements, emphasizing rapid deployment and mechanized operations designed to carry the battle into the rear of the enemy. To this was added an exceptional intelligence service, and a pronounced sensitivity to any change in the military capabilities of surrounding states.

In such circumstances, the line between forward defence and pre-emptive attack is easily transgressed, as it was in 1956, when Israel joined Britain and France in an effort to topple the government of Egypt; and again in 1967, when a series of ominous actions by Israel's neighbours provoked one of the most compelling demonstrations of *Blitzkrieg* yet seen. A key figure in both conflicts was Gamal Abdel Nasser, who came to power in Egypt following a military coup in 1952. Nasser's ascendancy was aided by Israel's victory, which radicalized the politics of the losers. Syria suffered a military coup a few months later, and did not achieve a stable government again until the arrival of Haffez Assad in 1970. In July 1951, King Abdulla of Jordan, the Arab leader most disposed to peace with Israel, was assassinated by an agent of the Mufti of Jerusalem. Nasser rose up on a similar wave of bitterness and humiliation. His aim, often stated, was to unite the Arab world behind his leadership, and transform Egypt into a power capable of effecting Israel's destruction.

The Suez Crisis of 1956 was precipitated by the convergence of Egypt's efforts at military and economic modernization. The previous year, Nasser had negotiated the withdrawal of British troops from the Suez Canal Zone. This disturbed the Israelis, who regarded the British presence as a check on Egyptian aggression. Egypt also obtained a massive shipment of arms from Czechoslovakia, thus providing the Soviet Union with its first major foothold in the region. This dismayed the US. The Israelis knew that Egypt sponsored terrorists working out of the Palestinian camps in the Gaza Strip, and chafed at Egypt's closure of the Strait of Tiran, a vital corridor for Israeli commerce. The US disliked being played against the Soviets, and in July 1956 withdrew funding for Nasser's pet development project, the Aswan Dam. Nasser responded by nationalizing the Suez Canal, whereupon the British and French, who had constructed it, prepared to take it back.

Israel was by then convinced that a major Egyptian attack was coming, and was planning to open the Strait of Tiran by seizing Sharm al-Sheikh. Yet it was reluctant to act without an ally. It found one when France approached David Ben-Gurion's government about participating in the operation it was developing with Britain. All three eventually

Block ships sunk at the entrance of the Suez Canal in Port Said, November 1956. The canal re-opened under Egyptian control in January 1957. Contrary to pre-war British claims, Egyptian pilots proved fully capable of guiding the world's ships through it.

agreed that Israel would mount an attack across the Sinai Peninsula, calculated to provide a pretext for British and French intervention along the canal.

All this misfired except the Israeli attack, which began on 29 October and swept the Egyptian Army out of the Sinai in five days. By the time British and French forces landed at Port Said on 5 November, however, international opinion, led by the US, had hardened against their action. A UN ceasefire was declared the next day, with the canal still in Egyptian hands. Nasser's prestige soared, despite his having been saved by the Americans. Israel achieved some of its objectives: the Strait of Tiran was opened, and terrorism from Gaza abated. But it had to give up the Sinai, and accept the reassurance afforded by UN peacekeepers in lieu of the Anglo-French cordon it had hoped to see between itself and its most dangerous enemy.

The peacekeepers were withdrawn at Nasser's insistence in May 1967, the climax of a series of moves not unlike those that preceded the 1956 war. Once again the Strait of Tiran was closed, this time in defiance of guarantees by the UN, the US, Britain and France, none of whom showed any sign of responding to Israeli pleas for assistance. Egypt, Jordan and Syria massed their forces along Israel's borders, and made military preparations whose object could only be Israel itself. Whether these actions were intended as preparation for war, or simply as an extraordinarily naïve exercise in coercive diplomacy, is disputed – though they were accompanied by the most vitriolic public statements, and created conditions that Israel had repeatedly declared to constitute *casus belli* in its eyes. These combined to drive Israeli opinion into a frenzy that no democratic government could realistically have been expected to resist, even had it wished to. The last straw was probably the dispatch of an Iraqi division to Jordan, a uniquely dangerous sector opposite Israel's narrow waist, where any setback was likely to prove irredeemable.

What became known as the Six Day War began on 5 June. The decisive stroke fell in the first few hours, when Israeli planes destroyed four-fifths of the Egyptian air force while it was still parked on the

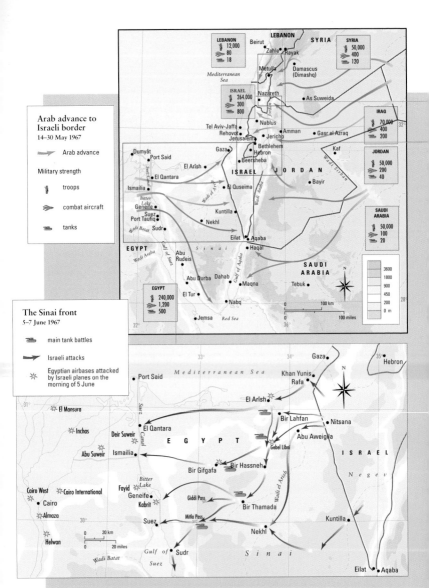

The map includes the following labels and legends:

Arab advance to Israeli border
14–30 May 1967

Arab advance

Military strength

troops

combat aircraft

tanks

LEBANON
12,000
80
18

SYRIA
50,000
400
120

ISRAEL
264,000
300
800

IRAQ
70,000
400
200

JORDAN
50,000
200
40

SAUDI ARABIA
50,000
100
20

EGYPT
240,000
1,200
500

Map place names (first/northern map): LEBANON, Beirut, Zahle, Rayak, SYRIA, Metulla, Damascus (Dimashq), Mediterranean Sea, ISRAEL, Nazareth, As Suweida, Tel Aviv-Jaffa, Rehovot, Nablus, Amman, Qasr el Azraq, Jerusalem, Bethlehem, Jericho, Kaf, Dumyât, Port Said, Gaza, Beersheba, Hebron, El Arîsh, JORDAN, Bayir, El Qantara, ISRAEL, Ismailia, El Quseima, Wadi Sirhan, Bitter Lake, Geneife, Kuntilla, Suez, Port Taufiq, Nekhl, Sudr, Eilat, Aqaba, Haqal, EGYPT, Abu Rudeis, Sinai, Gulf of Aqaba, SAUDI ARABIA, Abu Durba, Dahab, Magna, Tebuk, El Tur, Nabq, Jemsa, Red Sea

Scale: 3600, 1800, 900, 450, 200, 0 m; 0 100 km; 0 100 miles

The Sinai front
5–7 June 1967

main tank battles

Israeli attacks

Egyptian airbases attacked by Israeli planes on the morning of 5 June

Map place names (second/southern map): Gaza, Hebron, Mediterranean Sea, Khan Yunis, Rafa, Port Said, El Arîsh, El Mansura, Bir Lahfan, Nitsana, Inchas, El Qantara, Deir Suweir, EGYPT, Abu Aweigla, Gebel Libni, ISRAEL, Abu Suweir, Ismailia, Negev, Bir Hassneh, Bir Gifgafa, Cairo West, Cairo International, Fayid, Bitter Lake, Geneife, Giddi Pass, Wadi el Arish, Cairo, Kabrit, Bir Thamada, Almaza, Suez, Mitla Pass, Kuntilla, Helwan, Nekhl, Wadi Batat, Gulf of Suez, Sudr, Sinai, Eilat, Aqaba

Scale: 0 20 km; 0 20 miles

THE SINAI CAMPAIGN, 1967

Israeli objectives in the Sinai originally focused on the three critical passes at Giddi, Mitla and Bir Gifgafa. The subsequent advance of their forces to the east bank of the Suez Canal was an additional humiliation to the Egyptians, inflicted to no particular military purpose.

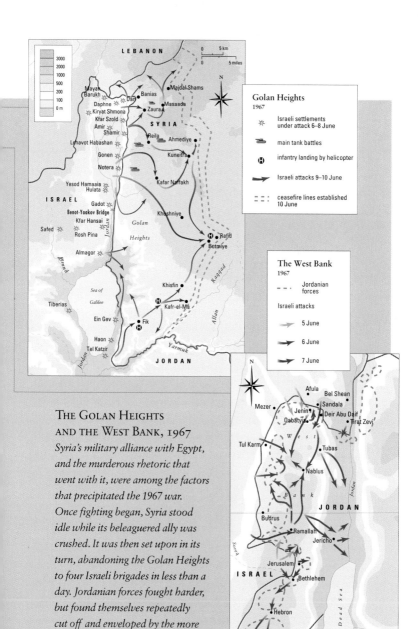

Golan Heights
1967

☀ Israeli settlements under attack 6–8 June

🚂 main tank battles

Ⓗ infantry landing by helicopter

➡ Israeli attacks 9–10 June

= = = ceasefire lines established 10 June

The West Bank
1967

– – – Jordanian forces

Israeli attacks

→ 5 June

➡ 6 June

➡ 7 June

The Golan Heights and the West Bank, 1967

Syria's military alliance with Egypt, and the murderous rhetoric that went with it, were among the factors that precipitated the 1967 war. Once fighting began, Syria stood idle while its beleaguered ally was crushed. It was then set upon in its turn, abandoning the Golan Heights to four Israeli brigades in less than a day. Jordanian forces fought harder, but found themselves repeatedly cut off and enveloped by the more agile Israelis.

tarmac. A similar fate would later befall Syria and Jordan, less excusably, given the proleptic demonstration against Egypt. The brilliance of this famous episode should not obscure the risks involved. If Egypt's planes had not been caught unawares – a critical contribution of Israeli military intelligence – or if the attack had miscarried for other reasons, both Israel's ground forces and its population would have been left naked to assault from the air. Once command of the air was achieved, however, results on the ground were virtually a foregone conclusion, despite the preponderance of men and *matériel* on the Arab side.

Israeli forces reached the Suez Canal on 8 June. By then a UN ceasefire was in place, though this did not deter the IDF from seizing the Golan Heights, from which Syrian guns had been bombarding northern Israel for twenty years. Half of Israel's casualties were suffered against its most reluctant opponent, Jordan, drawn into the fighting for fear of the political consequences of failing to maintain solidarity with its Arab neighbours. Diplomatic efforts to persuade Jordan to stand aside continued even after Jordanian guns began shelling Israeli positions on 5 June. Combat was most intense on this front because it was defended by the best of the Arab armies, the Arab Legion, trained by the British during the Mandate; and because the Israelis were unable to concentrate forces against Jordan until Egypt had been dealt with.

The results of the 1967 war alleviated the security problems created by Israel's small size and convoluted geometry. Israeli-controlled territory more than doubled thanks to its conquest of the West Bank, the Sinai and the Golan Heights, while the total length of its borders was reduced. Israeli cities were no longer within range of enemy guns, and the prospect of a fatal initial defeat was markedly reduced. Jordan's entry into the war also allowed Israel to take possession of those parts of Jerusalem from which Jews had been excluded since 1949, an accomplishment of no military significance, but with enormous emotional resonance, and not just among Jews. With all this,

Moshe Dayan, commander of the IDF during the 1956 war, and Defence Minister in 1967. He lost his eye as a Palmach company commander, fighting alongside the British against Vichy French forces in Syria in 1941.

Israel acquired direct responsibility for the displaced Palestinian populations on the West Bank and in the Gaza Strip. The fate of the Palestinian refugees had always presented the most fundamental challenge to Israel's legitimacy. This problem now resided within its own military frontiers.

The IDF's performance in 1967 was a feat of arms studied around the world. Yet it lacked the essential characteristic of a decisive victory, in that it failed to alter the political calculations of Israel's opponents. None of the Arab states who lost territory in the Six Day War was prepared to make peace in exchange for its return. Egypt felt humiliated by this new demonstration of Israeli military superiority, and waged a campaign of bombardments and raids across the Suez Canal that became known as the War of Attrition. It did not subside until August 1970, under pressure from the United States and the Soviet Union, whose roles as patrons of the main belligerents had become apparent since the Suez Crisis in 1956. Their influence would be decisive in concluding what would prove to be the final clash between Israel and Egypt three years later.

Nasser died six weeks after the War of Attrition ended. His successor, Anwar Sadat, lacked his predecessor's pan-Arabist ambitions. He also lacked the political standing necessary to conclude peace with Israel. The Yom Kippur War would be fought to acquire it. Although accompanied by conventionally inflated rhetoric – Sadat declared himself willing to sacrifice a million Egyptian lives to liberate the Sinai – the Egyptian attack had little prospect of advancing much beyond the east bank of the canal, owing to the dependence of Egyptian ground forces on the cover provided by anti-aircraft missile batteries of limited mobility, deployed on the canal's western side. The effective range of this defensive system did not reach the desert passes whose possession was necessary to any advance beyond a few miles. Within their lethal envelope, however, Egypt's surface-to-air missiles (SAMs) posed a formidable threat to Israeli planes. Over a hundred were shot down during the course of the war, compared to twenty-six in 1967. The other important new feature on the Egyptian side was

An Egyptian soldier celebrates the successful crossing of the Suez Canal. Getting back would prove a problem, but even so, the emotional lift provided by even limited success against the Israelis was indispensable to the making of peace later on.

The SA-6 'Gainful' was the Soviet Union's top-of-the-line surface-to-air missile. It posed a serious and unexpected threat to IAF pilots, who had learned to evade the older SA-2s, which could not hit targets below 150 feet. SA-6s deployed on mobile launchers, a feature the Egyptians did not exploit. None crossed the Suez Canal.

widespread use of portable anti-tank missiles, which for a time held Israel's armoured forces at bay.

In practice, the tactical advantages these new weapons afforded did not last more than a few days. Egyptian forces crossed the canal on 6 October, and achieved complete surprise. The date was chosen to take advantage of favourable tides, but it also coincided with the Jewish Day of Atonement, a fact that probably worked in the IDF's favour, since it insured the roads would be empty, and reservists at home. By nightfall on 9 October the front had stabilized, albeit at heavier cost than the Israelis had expected to pay against an adversary they had learned to disdain. On 14 October an Egyptian column advancing beyond SAM cover towards Sharm al-Sheikh was caught and annihilated, an early indication of how limited Egyptian prospects really were.

The next day an Israeli counter-attack began to crystallize opposite the command boundary of the 2nd and 3rd Egyptian Armies. Israeli troops crossed the canal there on 16 October, and had a secure

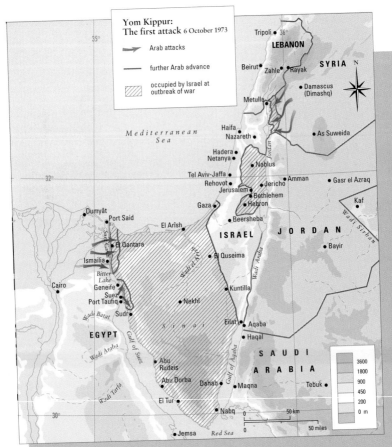

The Yom Kippur:
The first attack 6 October 1973

Arab attacks

further Arab advance

occupied by Israel at
outbreak of war

The Yom-Kippur War: the first attack 6 October 1973

The frontiers extended in 1967 became a tactical burden in 1973 because IDF units could not shift rapidly between fronts. Logistics were likewise strained by the protracted fighting on Sinai's far side. The speed with which Israeli equipment was consumed in 1973 alarmed NATO planners, who upped their estimate of the rate of attrition to be expected in a clash with the Warsaw Pact.

Opposite: The Golan Heights 6–24 October 1973

The Golan Heights became a graveyard for Syrian armour in 1973, despite the relatively weak Israeli forces deployed there. The slaughter resulted in large part from the extreme rigidity of Syrian doctrine. Once a company command tank was destroyed, the rest became sitting ducks.

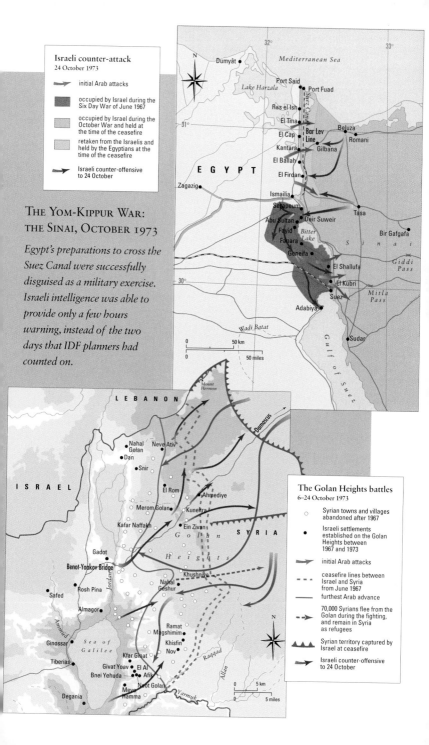

Israeli counter-attack
24 October 1973

→ initial Arab attacks

▨ occupied by Israel during the Six Day War of June 1967

▢ occupied by Israel during the October War and held at the time of the ceasefire

▢ retaken from the Israelis and held by the Egyptians at the time of the ceasefire

→ Israeli counter-offensive to 24 October

The Yom-Kippur War: the Sinai, October 1973

Egypt's preparations to cross the Suez Canal were successfully disguised as a military exercise. Israeli intelligence was able to provide only a few hours warning, instead of the two days that IDF planners had counted on.

Mediterranean Sea

Dumyât

Port Said • Port Fuad
Lake Harzala
Ras el Ish
El Tina
Bor Lev
Line
El Cap
Beluza
Romani
Kantara • Gilbana
El Ballah
El Firdan
Ismailia
Zagazig
E G Y P T
Serapeum
Abu Sultan • Deir Suweir
Tasa
Fayid • *Bitter* • Bir Gafgafa
Fanara • *Lake*
Geneifa • S i n a i
Giddi Pass
El Shallufa
El Kubri
Suez • *Mitla Pass*
Adabiya

Wadi Batat

0 ____ 50 km
0 ____ 50 miles

Sudar

Gulf of Suez

L E B A N O N

Mount Hermon

Damascus

Nahal Golan
Neve Ativ
Dan
Snir
El Rom
Ahmediye
Merom Golan • Kuneitra
Kafar Naffakh • Ein Zivan
G o l a n
I S R A E L
Gadot
H e i g h t s
S Y R I A
Benot-Yaakov Bridge
Khushniya
Rosh Pina
Nahal Geshur
Safed
Almagor
Ginossar • *Sea of Galilee*
Ramat Magshimim
Khisfin
Tiberias
Kfar Givat • Nov
Givat Yoav • El Al
Bnei Yehuda • Afik
Neot Golan
Degania
Mevo Hamma

Jordan
Amud
Raqqad
Allan
Yarmuk

The Golan Heights battles
6–24 October 1973

○ Syrian towns and villages abandoned after 1967

● Israeli settlements established on the Golan Heights between 1967 and 1973

→ initial Arab attacks

--- ceasefire lines between Israel and Syria from June 1967

— furthest Arab advance

⇢ 70,000 Syrians flee from the Golan during the fighting, and remain in Syria as refugees

▲▲▲ Syrian territory captured by Israel at ceasefire

→ Israeli counter-offensive to 24 October

0 ____ 5 km
0 ____ 5 miles

bridgehead a day after that. IDF ground operations destroyed the Egyptian missile defences, after which the Israeli air force again commanded the air over the battlefield. By the time a UN-imposed ceasefire became effective on 24 October, the 3rd Egyptian Army had been enveloped west of the canal, and Russian airborne units were preparing to rescue them. The US responded by placing all its forces on alert worldwide, a perilous moment indeed, but a fleeting one.

Egypt's attack had been co-ordinated with one by Syria, a diversion in the larger scheme of things, but dangerous because of the proximity of the Golan Heights to Israeli cities. Syria committed over five divisions and 1,200 tanks to the assault, which was designed to exploit a dilemma created by the IDF's victory six years before: Israel's frontiers were now sufficiently extended that it was not possible to move forces rapidly from one front to another. Syria's attack was thus met by two isolated

Israeli soldiers resting on top of the enormous sand embankment built along the Suez Canal by Israel after 1967. This unusual structure was part of a defensive system known as the Bar Lev Line. The embankment was built as an obstacle, but mainly to obstruct the Egyptian view of Israeli movements. Egyptian forces cut through it in short order in 1973, using high pressure hoses mounted on barges in the canal.

Israeli brigades, which sacrificed themselves in the course of inflicting staggering losses on their assailants – almost nine hundred Syrian tanks were destroyed or abandoned in the course of the fighting.

Even so, some mystery remains as to why the Syrian advance was broken off, as it was, on 8 October, after which the IDF regained, and improved upon, the positions achieved in 1967. A few scholars have suggested that Israel threatened Syria with nuclear attack. Israel had embarked upon a nuclear weapons programme with French assistance in the 1950s, and Egyptian planners later claimed they believed Israel possessed up to a dozen atomic bombs when they were preparing their own operation in 1973. Israeli Prime Minister Shimon Peres hinted in his memoirs that Israel possessed such weapons even in 1967, but was dissuaded from publicizing them to deter the Arabs because the US had set its face against nuclear proliferation. None of this is impossible, though the Egyptian claim that the Yom Kippur War was launched in defiance of Israeli nuclear arms suggests Peres was too generous in his estimate of their deterrent value.

Despite the desperate state to which Egyptian forces had been reduced at the end of the Yom Kippur War, its larger results served Egyptian interests well, and Israel's too. The honour of Egyptian arms had been restored – the subsequent, negotiated pull back of Israeli forces from the east bank of the canal could be represented as a reconquest – while shortcomings were discounted against the enormous reputation the IDF had enjoyed since 1967. The war demonstrated that Israel was not invincible, and also, paradoxically, that it could not be overthrown militarily. Both inferences were reinforced by the emphatic reactions of the Soviet Union and the United States to the prospect that a genuinely decisive shift in the balance of power in the region might be in the offing, as it was during the few hours when Egypt's 3rd Army was at the mercy of the IDF.

In these circumstances, real peace became possible, though it would take years to achieve. The Camp David Accords were signed in 1978, and created the framework for a final settlement the following year,

The Camp David Accords were the first peace treaty between Israel and any of its Arab neighbours. Left to right: Egypt's President Anwar Sadat, President Jimmy Carter of the United States, and Israeli Prime Minister Menachem Begin.

under which the Sinai was returned to Egypt, and normal diplomatic relations established. Although hatred of Israel would remain endemic within the Arab world – Sadat's conclusion of peace would cost him his life two years later at the hands of a Muslim extremist – Egypt's withdrawal from the coalition of forces arrayed against the Jewish State ensured its survival, if not its tranquillity.

The most intractable problem arising from Israel's existence has been to secure a decent life for the Palestinians displaced by the 1948 war, which they know simply as 'the catastrophe'. Although Palestinian rights have featured in the public pronouncements of Israel's Arab opponents, none can plausibly be said to have fought for them. Under the Mandate, the term 'Palestinian' was used mainly by Jews and

A Palestinian man, armed with a nail-studded potato, prepares to attack Israeli troops. The paltry nature of the weapon says a good deal about the determination of the person preparing to throw it.

Westerners, not Arabs. Had the Yishuv been destroyed, the result would almost certainly have been the partition of Jewish territory among Egypt, Syria and Jordan. Palestinian national identity is thus a product, rather than a cause, of Arab–Jewish hostility. It has been overwhelmingly shaped by the brutal experiences of internment and exile, and by the terrorism conducted by groups purporting to represent Palestinian interests.

Among these, the one that would achieve general international recognition was the Palestine Liberation Organization (PLO), established in 1964 as an umbrella organization for a number of clandestine resistance groups. The most important was Fatah, one of whose founders, Yasser Arafat, became chairman of the PLO in 1969. The PLO's commitment to armed struggle made it a danger to surrounding Arab states, which provided bases and financial support for its activities, only to find their own stability undermined by the Palestinian presence. Arafat's forces were driven out of Jordan and into Lebanon in 1970, where their activities contributed to the onset of civil war five years later. Israel chased the PLO out of Beirut in 1982 (after which the IDF would occupy southern Lebanon, to no particular advantage, for eighteen years). Thereafter the PLO would be based in Tunis, and, from 1987, in Baghdad as well. Its peripatetic and ineffectual existence created much strain within the Palestinian leadership, which became progressively disconnected from the lives of the people, above all those living in the camps on the West Bank and the Gaza Strip.

These rose up, starting in 1987, in a series of riots, strikes and demonstrations known collectively as the *intifada* ('shaking off'), a movement directed against the Israeli occupation established twenty years before, and also against the cynicism of the Arab world towards the Palestinian plight. The *intifada* presented a serious challenge to Arafat's leadership, at a time when the winding down of the Cold War was leaving the PLO increasingly isolated. He responded by renouncing terrorism (for which he had never accepted responsibility in any case), and proclaiming the existence of a Palestinian government in exile, with himself at its head. These actions, which attracted widespread international endorsement, entailed recognition of Israel's existence, a crucial requirement for the onset of negotiations. Progress would be agonizingly slow, however, owing to persisting Israeli suspicions that have been kept alive by persisting terrorism, which the PLO has failed to control. Although the world has recognized the PLO's authority to act for the Palestinians, there are many unappeasably violent elements within the Palestinian diaspora that have not. In any event, the basic deal worked out between Israel and Egypt at Camp David, and embodied in a number of UN resolutions, has not changed: land for peace. The Israelis have the land. It remains to be seen if the Palestinians have anything to trade.

CHAPTER EIGHT

Vietnam

Some wars produce iconic images of combat that capture the essence of the struggle as a whole. In the First World War it was the mass attack across no man's land; in the Second World War the mechanized battle. In Vietnam it was the ambush. Shown here, the aftermath of one such attack in War Zone C, Vietnam, 1965.

Vietnam

The country at this time took ye Alarm, and were immediately
in Arms, and had taken their different stations behind Walls, on
our Flanks, and thus we were harassed in our Front, Flanks, and
Rear … it not being possible for us to meet a man otherwise
than behind a Bush, Stone hedge, or Tree, who immediately
gave his fire and went off.

A British officer at Lexington, Massachusetts, 1775

THE PARTITION OF Vietnam in 1954 imposed a pause upon serious
fighting that lasted five years. The Viet Minh were exhausted by
the struggle against the French, and needed time to consolidate their
rule. This involved such conspicuous brutality that Ho would
eventually issue a public apology, while Giap noted privately that 'many
honest people were executed', and that 'torture came to be regarded as
a normal part of the party organization'. As many as a million
Northerners fled to the South, against perhaps 80,000 going the other
way. Ho in any case did not expect that further war would be necessary
to unify Vietnam. He judged his Southern counterpart, Diem, to be the
last in a long line of ineffectual puppets. Yet Diem proved reasonably
adept. He certainly recognized the pointlessness of harbouring designs
against Ho's regime. On the contrary, neither he nor his American
backers had any intention of allowing the national election called for
by the Geneva Settlement to take place. For some years after the
deadline passed in 1956, however, the North confined itself to political
subversion in the South, in part because the Chinese and the Soviets
would not support more forceful action.

Diem responded with increasing repression, and ham-fisted efforts
at anti-communist indoctrination. The latter availed little: in the
Southern countryside the communists were remembered as the ones
who fought the French and the Japanese when no one else did.
Nevertheless, Diem's efforts put sufficient pressure on his communist

opponents that additional measures to support them became necessary. In 1959, Ho's government formed two special groups to organize infiltration, one overland via what became known as the Ho Chi Minh Trail, the other from the sea. The National Liberation Front (NLF) was founded the following year to conduct guerrilla war in the South. Dubbed 'Vietcong' ('Vietnamese communists') by Diem, its dependence upon Hanoi was deprecated. It presented itself as a democratic and anti-American organization, and included some non-communists in its ranks.

The United States responded by establishing Military Assistance Command Vietnam (MACV) in February 1962. Its mission was to train the South Vietnamese Army (ARVN), and promote pacification

The People's Army of Vietnam on the march in Hanoi. The military mobilization of North Vietnamese society was indispensable to the communist victory. The South eventually tried to match the effort, but the results, while similar on the parade ground, looked different on the battlefield.

measures designed to bolster Diem's regime. It soon discovered that off-the-shelf methods of counter-insurgency did not necessarily work in Vietnam. An early attempt to resettle the rural population in secure 'strategic hamlets', modelled on British programmes in Malaya and Kenya, misfired, because the US failed to take account of the emotional bonds that Vietnamese peasants felt towards the soil on which they lived, and in which their ancestors were often buried; also because ARVN forces showed no inclination to take the risks necessary to protect the hamlets. Their regular penetration by NLF recruiters and terrorists became a further humiliation for the government. The failure of the strategic hamlets was symptomatic of a larger difficulty the US and its South Vietnamese ally had in grasping the impact of the war on the rural population. Over the

A strategic hamlet in the central highlands of Vietnam. The village perimeter is surrounded by three fences and a ditch. The larger huts are ringed by additional fences of their own.

course of the war, over half of all South Vietnamese peasants would be displaced from their homes at least once. For many, the first such experience was being moved into a strategic hamlet. In the eyes of the average Southern farmer, they amounted to Potemkin villages surrounded by American barbed wire, and guarded by soldiers whose first concern was their own skins.

Apart from intense anti-communism, the outstanding feature of Diem's regime was corruption. Diem was by temperament an autocrat, and by upbringing an urban Catholic in a country whose population was mainly rural and Buddhist. His capacity to inspire distrust was far-reaching. He became the target of repeated coups, and the final crisis that brought him down was precipitated not by the NLF, but by Buddhist monks setting fire to themselves to protest the intrusion of security forces into their temples and monasteries. He ruled through family members and cronies, chiefly other Catholics driven south by Ho's victory. None of the members of Diem's inner circle were born in South Vietnam. Nevertheless, Diem was almost unique among non-communist nationalists in being untainted by collaboration during the world war, a minimum requirement for political credibility when the country was partitioned. Later the US concluded that he could not bring stability to the South, and acquiesced in his overthrow (though not his assassination) by a clique of generals in November 1963. Yet no more capable figure ever emerged. The fecklessness and venality of the South Vietnamese regime became as proverbial as the ruthless cruelty of the North, and contributed to the demoralization of the Americans who would be sent to fight for it.

The decision to send them followed a series of escalatory moves by the North in 1964, which convinced the United States that the South was about to lose the war. Until the Tet Offensive in 1968, if not, indeed, until the last Americans left four years later, the image of victory preoccupying the minds of Northern leaders was that of a general uprising in the South. Ho expected one to follow Diem's overthrow. When it failed to materialize, infiltration was stepped up. By mid summer the NLF controlled four-fifths of the Vietnamese countryside, and often outnumbered the ARVN units it engaged. Saigon tried to strike back. On 30 July South Vietnamese commandos began covert maritime raiding against the North, a secret operation that gave rise, a few days later, to an attack by North Vietnamese torpedo boats on the American destroyer *Maddox*, which was gathering intelligence in the Tonkin Gulf. The United States Congress responded by authorizing 'all necessary measures to repel armed attack against the forces of the United States and to prevent further aggression'. By then a retaliatory strike had already been carried out by carrier aircraft, and further action was delayed to avoid impacting the presidential election in November. In the meantime, regular units of North Vietnam's PAVN (People's Army of Vietnam) had begun moving below the 17th Parallel for the first time, an indication that, in the eyes of the North, victory was at hand.

The American war in Vietnam began in earnest in the winter of 1965, reached its peak following the NLF's Tet Offensive in 1968, and concluded with the negotiated withdrawal of American forces in 1973. It had three basic components: a strategic air campaign; conventional ground operations by forces as large as an army corps; and a variety of measures aimed at counter-insurgency, nation-building and civil pacification. These elements harmonized imperfectly with each other. In particular, the intense and indiscriminate violence of main force 'search and destroy' operations, as they became known, comported ill with the requirements of pacification. Yet there was no question of a Northern victory as long as they continued. Beyond averting the South's defeat, however, lay the question of ensuring its legitimacy and survival once the Americans had gone. This problem, foreseeable by all concerned, proved insoluble, since American tactical success, while necessary to its accomplishment, was not sufficient to bring it about. North Vietnam would often be driven to the brink of despair by the scale of violence directed against it by the

A US war plane shot down north of Hanoi, moments before impact. The pilot's parachute is visible in the upper right. A North Vietnamese with a rifle awaits his descent.

US, but there never seems to have been a moment when Hanoi thought the South could endure for long on its own.

Strategic bombardment always loomed large in the American conception of how to make war in Vietnam. Planning for an air campaign against the North antedated the Tonkin Gulf Resolution by several months, a fact revealed to general chagrin by the publication of the *Pentagon Papers* in 1971. Sustained bombing began in February, ostensibly in reprisal for NLF attacks on American bases in the South. The campaign, called Rolling Thunder, was designed to achieve psychological and political, rather than strictly military effects, by inflicting gradually increasing punishment. At first the target list was limited to military bases and logistical targets along the Ho Chi Minh Trail, and near the demilitarized zone separating North and South. Over time it would expand to include factories, fuel storage facilities and transportation infrastructure throughout the country. Although the escalatory nature of the plan would later be criticized, the alternative − a campaign that struck harder at the outset − was not obviously more promising, given the dearth of strategically significant targets in the North. A more concerted attack would still have been based on nothing more than psychological speculation about how best to impact enemy morale. To the extent that the Northern war effort depended upon an industrial and logistical infrastructure, its crucial nodes were in China and the Soviet Union, and were thus immune from direct attack.

Area bombing of Northern cities was ruled out; but as the target list expanded, civilian suffering did too. The CIA estimated that 2,800 North Vietnamese were killed each month in 1967. Hanoi always assumed a city-busting campaign was just around the corner, and took pains to disburse and protect its population. Many Northerners spent years living underground. In time, the North acquired formidable air defences, chiefly MIGs and SAMs from the Soviet Union, which felt that its credibility as the guardian of world communism was threatened by the American attack. Over nine hundred US planes were shot down in the course of delivering 643,000 tons of bombs against the North, far more than were dropped on Japan in 1944–5. In monetary terms, the cost of Rolling Thunder exceeded the value of the things it destroyed by a factor of ten. It also

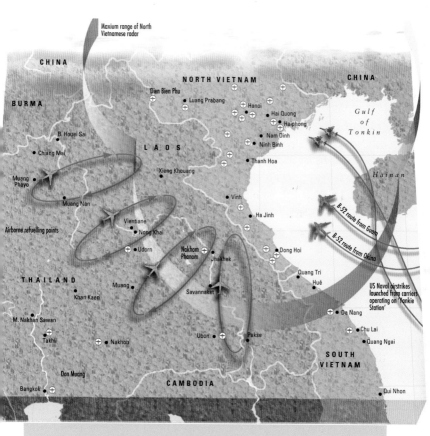

Maxium range of North
Vietnamese radar

CHINA

BURMA

NORTH VIETNAM

Dien Bien Phu
• Luang Prabang
Hanoi
• Hai Quong
Haiphong
• Nam Dinh
• Ninh Binh

CHINA

Gulf
of
Tonkin

B. Houei Sai
• Chiang Mai

L A O S

Xieng Khouang

Hainan

Muang
Phayo
Muang Nan

• Vinh

Airborne refuelling points

Vientiane
• Nong Khai

• Ha Jinh

Udorn

Nakhom
Phanom
Jhakhek

Dong Hoi

B-52 route from Guam
B-52 route from Okina

T H A I L A N D

Muang
Khan Kaen

Savannaket

Quang Tri
Hué

US Naval airstrikes
launched from carriers
operating on 'Yankie
Station'

M. Nakhan Sawan

Takhli
• Nakhou

Ubon
Pakse

• Da Nang

• Chu Lai
• Quang Ngai

Don Muang

Bangkok

CAMBODIA

SOUTH
VIETNAM

Qui Nhon

ROLLING THUNDER

In 1961 Curtis Le May, Chief of Staff of the United States Air Force, testified before Congress that American air doctrine had not changed since the formation of the US Army's Air General Headquarters in 1935. Vietnam proved him right.

Rolling Thunder
2 March 1965–31 October 1968

⊕   North Vietnamese airfields

⊕   US and allied airfields

failed in its role as a signalling mechanism. The US suspended its bombing of the North seven times between 1965 and 1968, in a vain effort to communicate its willingness to negotiate. Hanoi used the breaks to rebuild and rearm.

A North Vietnamese civilian prepares for attack from the air. The North claimed to have dug 30,000 miles of tunnels in an effort to protect its population from American bombers.

US ground forces were first introduced into South Vietnam in March 1965 in the form of two Marine battalions detailed to provide security for the airbase at Da Nang. They became the thin edge of an army that within three years would exceed half a million. Their purpose, as envisioned by MACV's commander, William Westmoreland, was to fight a war of attrition based upon superior firepower, a task he judged the ARVN incapable of performing for lack of aggressive leadership. It was a concept deeply rooted in American military doctrine, tradition and prejudice, and was executed with much skill and determination but to limited effect. Search and destroy missions were designed to eradicate opposing forces within predefined territorial areas, normally by establishing some sort of blocking position or free-fire zone on to which enemy units would be driven. Because the territory so cleared was not held, however, American forces were condemned to scour the same countryside again and again, measuring their accomplishments in terms of Vietnamese dead, a number that inevitably came to include any civilians caught in the fighting. Because the other side knew that it would be able to regain almost any position thus lost, its forces were free to evade the worst of whatever the Americans had in store.

American forces inflicted savage losses on NLF and PAVN units with which they made contact. Yet, even within the framework of offensive ground operations, such contact was almost always initiated by the communists, itself striking testimony to the fury inspired by the American presence. Vietnam might easily have evolved into an endless contest between helicopters and booby traps. It did not do so because of the determination of the North to see the Americans off in good time, despite the additional suffering this entailed. The enemy's aggressiveness was matched by his elusiveness. Over the course of the war, about 85 per cent of American ordnance was expended in 'unobserved' fire. Yet it all came down somewhere, occasionally in one piece: one estimate concluded that unexploded American bombs and shells alone provided those brave enough to retrieve them with enough explosives to kill 1,000 men per year. In the final analysis, the 'body count' obtained by American forces had to be measured against the raw ability of the North to replace its losses. Roughly 200,000 North Vietnamese males reached draft age every year during the war. Even the United States was unable to kill that many on a sustained basis. Supposing it had been, it is still difficult to imagine a more demoralizing theory of victory for a strong, rich country at war with a small, poor one.

MACV's main force operations sought to exploit American firepower, tactical proficiency and logistics. It regarded pacification, civic action and the suppression of what became known as the 'Vietcong infrastructure' as chiefly the responsibility of the South Vietnamese Army, backed by constabulary forces nicknamed 'Ruff-

Puffs' (RF-PF, Regional Forces-Popular Forces). This division of labour made basic sense, though it was not necessarily attractive to ARVN officers, who felt that they had been elbowed aside by their imperious ally. Neither was it absolute. One important exception was the Marine Corps Combined Action Platoons (CAPs), which were set up permanently in individual towns and villages along the heavily populated coast. The CAPs employed classic 'ink blot' counter-insurgency techniques to clear and hold the countryside around their positions. They attracted criticism within MACV for their apparent lack of aggressiveness in seeking out the enemy, while earning the gratitude of those who enjoyed their protection. The real difficulty with the CAPs' approach, however, was not that it lacked offensive punch, but that it was being executed by Americans. Such efforts did nothing to build confidence in the regime in Saigon; rather the contrary.

After May 1967, American and South Vietnamese pacification efforts were centralized under a civilian agency called CORDS (Civil

LINES OF SUPPLY IN SOUTH VIETNAM
1959–72

The key to Northern communications with the South was a network of roads and paths winding through Laos and Cambodia, known as the Ho Chi Minh Trail. Although American bombing would sometimes reduce the flow of men and supplies along it to a trickle, that was enough to keep the NLF insurgency alive. The crucial choke point for American logistics early in the war was South Vietnamese harbours, which could not accommodate deep draught vessels. A more rapid build-up of American forces would have been difficult as a consequence.

Lines of supply in
South Vietnam 1959–72

former French colony

Communist-held areas

Ho Chi Minh Trail

infiltration by sea

Sihanouk trail

Communist attacks

main supply base

US air base, with date

Operations and Revolutionary Development Support), which operated alongside MACV, in co-operation with the CIA and the Agency for International Development. Its chief accomplishment was to expand and equip South Vietnamese militia, including the Ruff-Puffs and a new group called the People's Self-Defense Forces. Collectively, popular forces in the South would eventually number in the millions, though their training was often rudimentary, and morale correspondingly low. CORDS was also responsible for the Phoenix Program, an operation much feared by the NLF because it proceeded by targeting and, in rare but notorious instances, assassinating important cadres singled out by US and Vietnamese intelligence. These paramilitary programmes were supplemented by social reform, of which the most impressive was a massive land redistribution project in the Mekong delta, concluded in 1970, whereby 2.5 million acres of land were purchased from large landowners and given to formerly landless tenants.

In the wake of America's defeat, its Secretary of State, Henry Kissinger, would compare the insurgency in South Vietnam to a cape in the hands of a matador – the North – which the US exhausted itself attacking, only to discover too late that its true nemesis stood off to one side, sword in hand. His remark misrepresents America's strategic outlook, which always assumed that revolution in the South would die on the vine once Northern support was cut off. It also points to a large and fruitless controversy over which of America's ground wars – the war of the big battalions, or of pacification and counter-insurgency – was the 'real' one, and which a useless diversion of resources. It is in its way analogous to the question of whether the Viet Minh were 'really' communists or nationalists, and is equally naïve. MACV, having committed itself to statistical measures of its

Fire support base Charlie One, just below the DMZ. The 175mm (M107) self-propelled gun at centre left had an effective range of 20 miles.

own effectiveness (e.g. 'body count'), also kept close track of what the other side was up to. Its numbers, summarized below, tell the story surprisingly well.

NLF / PAVN attacks	1965	1966	1967	1968	1969	1970	1971	1972
Battalion or larger	73	44	54	126	34	13	2	106
Small units	612	862	1,484	1,374	1,581	1,757	1,613	2,323
Indirect fire	—	—	16,494	15,845	16,049	14,557	8,691	13,013
Kidnap, murder, etc.	—	—	7,566	9,716	10,638	12,056	9,973	8,906

One sees here a single war fought in two registers. Underneath was a *guerrilla* war that never seriously slackened once the American build-up was achieved in 1967. Upon this were superimposed three concerted attempts to inflict heavier blows. The first came in 1965, and coincided with the arrival of American ground forces. The last, in 1972, proved to be a premature attempt to exploit their departure. In between lay the Tet Offensive of 1968.

The central feature of Tet was a co-ordinated assault by the NLF on the urban areas of South Vietnam, which had seen little hard fighting up to then. Although the precise reasoning behind the offensive remains a mystery, it appears to have been conceived in a spirit of unrealistic optimism not unlike that which inspired the Viet Minh's Red River campaign in 1951. Giap, who bore responsibility for both operations, would later claim that the goal of Tet was to discredit the Saigon government in the eyes of its own people, and that the profound reaction it inspired among Americans was unanticipated.

The attacks against the cities were timed to coincide with the lunar new year, an important Vietnamese holiday that in previous years had been marked by an informal truce. They were also preceded by multiple diversionary operations against American positions in the central highlands and below the demilitarized zone. These feints worked because they appealed to American preconceptions about how and where major military actions would occur, and because they seemed designed to re-create the Viet Minh's epic success at Dien Bien Phu. Although US intelligence accumulated much evidence suggesting a move against Southern cities was in the works, such an attack was judged to have no purpose except to distract attention from the real battle raging to the north.

US forces race towards helicopters sent to pull them out of a firefight. Air mobility afforded considerable advantages to US forces in Vietnam, but did not entirely negate the superior foot mobility of the other side.

On 30–31 January, NLF forces struck simultaneously against a hundred district and provincial capitals in the South, five of six autonomous cities (including Saigon) and dozens of hamlets. ARVN headquarters in Saigon came under fire for several hours, as did the presidential palace and the American embassy. Most attacks were beaten off in a few days, though it took almost a month to recapture the old imperial capital at Hué. Tet was also preceded by a major PAVN assault on the Marine base at Khe Sanh, which began on 21 January. This operation was too large to be considered diversionary, and may have been intended to open an avenue for PAVN forces to advance en masse into the South, should the Tet attacks inspire the long-hoped-for

THE TET OFFENSIVE: BATTLE FOR HUÉ JANUARY–FEBRUARY 1968

The heaviest fighting of the Tet Offensive took place in the old imperial capital of Hué. The city had seen no serious combat until then, and was lightly defended by elements of the ARVN 1st Division. Clearing the city required intense house-to-house fighting, supported by air strikes and naval gunfire. About 50 per cent of Hué's buildings were destroyed or damaged in the battle. US and South Vietnamese forces suffered almost 3,800 casualties, of which 600 were fatal. Communist dead were estimated at 5,000.

1. 31 January, 3.30 am: the North Vietnamese 6th Infantry Regiment, backed by the Vietcong 12th Sapper Battalion, launch a rocket barrage followed by an infantry assault on the old imperial citadel. The North Vietnamese and Vietcong quickly capture the citadel

2. Midday: ARVN 1st Division hold on to their headquarters compound on the north-eastern edge of the citadel

3. Evening: South Vietnamese reinforcements arrive and begin to retake the citadel

4. US and South Vietnamese fly constant air support missions

5. 2 February: the US Army's 3rd Brigade establish blocking positions to prevent supplies reaching the North Vietnamese within the citadel

6. 4 February: two US Marine battalions attempt to clear the south bank of infiltrators, fighting house to house

7. Elements of three North Vietnamese divisions attempt to infiltrate the city. Fighting continues

8. 21 February: South Vietnamese forces fight southward through the citadel linking up with US forces heading north and east. They launch a co-ordinated attack on the remaining Vietcong positions. Fighting ends on 2 March

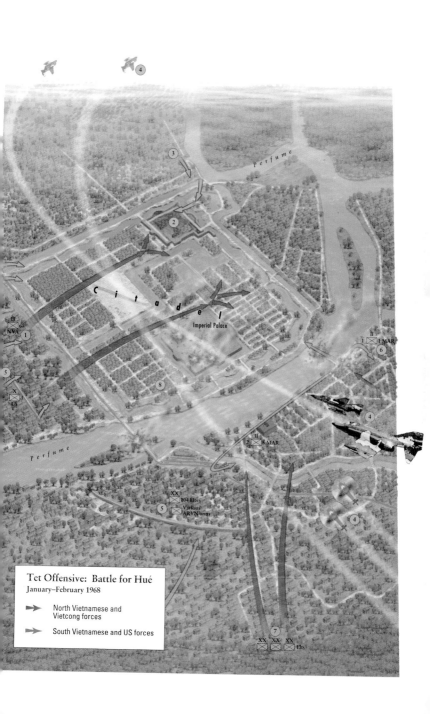

Citadel

Imperial Palace

Perfume

Perfume

104 Elts
Various
ARVN units

I ⊠ 1 MAR
6

II
2 ⊠ 5 MAR

III
6
NVA
1

X
US
5

XX
5

XX XX XX
7   Elts

Tet Offensive: Battle for Hué
January–February 1968

➤ North Vietnamese and
Vietcong forces

➤ South Vietnamese and US forces

THE UNSEEN ENEMY

About 11 per cent of US fatalities in Vietnam (and 17 per cent of wounds) were inflicted by mines and booby traps, compared to 4 per cent in the Second World War and Korea. Common traps included tripwires attached to explosives or spiked mud balls, which would swing down from a tree and impale the victim; a single machine-gun bullet buried upright, with its primer cap resting on a nail; and pits full of Punji stakes. The sense of hidden peril was heightened by the NLF's reliance on mazes of subterranean tunnels for movement, refuge, and storage. Traps and tunnels often went together, since one important use for the former was to defend bases and bivouac areas from the enemy's unexpected approach. Traps were also set in places where troops might throw themselves down to avoid incoming fire, for example the ditches alongside a road.

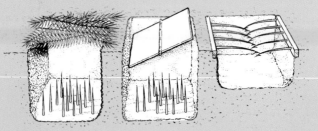

ABOVE: *Punji stakes were the most common form of trap used in Vietnam. Designs like the one on the right became common after the United States introduced combat boots with steel-reinforced soles.*

general uprising there. The siege of Khe Sanh lasted seventy-seven days. By the time it was over, the NLF position in South Vietnam had been destroyed, and the US had decided to withdraw from the war.

Tet exposed strategic illusions on both sides. It demonstrated that the South Vietnamese were not going to throw off their government and turn themselves over to Hanoi. No general uprising could be expected. In any event, the chief instrument for bringing one about, the

Vietnamese women sharpening bamboo to make Punji stakes. The stakes were often fire-hardened to aid penetration, and tipped with excrement to induce infection.

NLF, had exposed itself to the light of day in its attacks upon the cities, and suffered irrecoverable losses as a consequence. Had the US been in a position to exploit the tactical success that Hanoi's gamble delivered to it, Tet might have constituted a considerable setback for the North, though scarcely a decisive one. As it was, however, the US had no coherent military strategy into which its somewhat fortuitous victory could be fitted.

The fact that the Tet Offensive occurred at all was deeply shocking to American opinion, which had been deliberately misled by Washington about the progress of the war. Much would later be made of the fact that American journalists, taken by surprise like everyone else by the scale of the communist attack, cast the NLF's actions in too favourable a light, and failed to convey the scale of the defeat it finally suffered. Be that as it may, the real effect of Tet was to let the American public in on unpleasant facts long familiar to those responsible for the war: specifically that current American methods were producing marginal results at best; and that any improvement would require much larger forces and many more years of fighting. Frustration and disillusionment were well advanced among American civilian and military decision-makers by the end of 1967. Tet helped the rest of the country catch up.

On 31 March 1968, the US President, Lyndon Johnson, announced that he would not seek re-election, halted American bombing north of the 20th Parallel – a proscription later expanded to all of the North – and renewed a long-standing American offer to negotiate a settlement to the war. Preliminary discussions began in Paris in May, but quickly stalled, since neither side was prepared to make concessions based on the military results achieved to that point. The United States drew a line

under its war effort when it publicly rejected a request from MACV to increase American ground forces by 40 per cent. Yet it was far from accepting defeat, and feared the loss of credibility and prestige that might follow the abandonment of its South Vietnamese ally. The North undoubtedly accepted the American offer not because it expected to reach agreement, but because it thought talks would provide another avenue by which pressure could be brought to bear on American and international opinion. The year after Tet thus proved to be the bloodiest of the entire war, as both sides fought to improve their positions.

The USS New Jersey *firing into the DMZ, 30 September 1968. The majority of North Vietnamese targets struck from the air during the war were also within range of the 16-inch guns of Iowa-class battleships like the* New Jersey, *an alternative that entailed no risk to air crews.*

Under any circumstances, serious discussions would have had to await the results of the 1968 presidential election, won by Richard Nixon partly on the strength of a promise of 'peace with honor'. Nixon was no more willing than his predecessor to bear the humiliation of forsaking Saigon, though having had no share in the decisions to send American forces to Vietnam he was able to start bringing them out. American troop levels began to decline in June 1969, and were cut in half – to 280,000 – by the end of 1970, and in half

A US Army Huey UH-1D, customized for defoliation, applies Agent Orange in the Mekong delta. Chemical herbicides were used to clear jungle and, less extensively, to destroy crops in areas thought to be controlled by the NLF. Over 5 million acres were sprayed in the course of the war.

again in 1971. In practice, American disengagement was more rapid than these figures suggest, because American forces ceased to be committed to major ground operations once the withdrawals had begun. This policy, known as Vietnamization, proved an awkward basis for negotiation, since Hanoi's fondest wish was certain to be granted whether it made any concessions or not.

As in Korea, expressions of American resolve would be delivered mainly from the air, most persistently through the 'secret' bombing – of communist bases and logistics in Laos and Cambodia. These operations, which extended from 1969 to 1973, proved profoundly destructive of social order and political authority in both countries, without perceptibly impacting the Northern war effort, or, for that matter, the negotiations in Paris.

Better results were achieved against the North's 'Easter Offensive' of 1972, in which the equivalent of twenty PAVN divisions – its entire effective strength – was committed in a three-pronged attack meant to compel the South's surrender. The Easter Offensive was a strictly conventional operation, in which the main work was done by Soviet-supplied tanks and artillery. It was met on the ground by ARVN units that fell back everywhere but did not break, thus allowing American planes to be brought to bear against precisely the sorts of concentrated, high-value targets they had been designed on the drawing board to

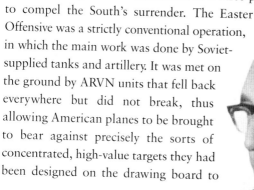

American Secretary of State Henry Kissinger bore chief responsibility for devising a form of words capable of extricating the United States from Vietnam. His interlocutor, Le Duc Tho, refused his share of their joint Nobel Peace Prize in 1973.

Two UPI reporters share a trench with ARVN soldiers during the siege of Quang Tri in 1972. The stab-in-the-back legend that attached to US media coverage of the war did not necessarily extend to combat journalists, who often ran great risks to get their stories.

destroy. The result was a defeat from which the PAVN would not recover for three years. The US also resumed its strategic air campaign against the North on an unprecedented scale, and mined the North's harbours, a severe blow, given that nearly all supplies from China and the Soviet Union arrived by sea. In all, Giap's effort to force the pace of what should have been a foreseeable victory must count as the most colossal miscalculation in the history of the Vietnamese Revolution. Yet it was not enough to deprive the North of ultimate success.

America's fury abated in October 1972. A few weeks later Secretary of State Kissinger went on television to declare that 'peace was at hand'. This was a ruse designed to cover a breakdown in negotiations, brought about by the objections of South Vietnam's president, Nguyen Van Thieu, to some details in the agreement Kissinger had worked out with the communists. Hanoi, feeling betrayed, refused to budge further. The result was a final round of air strikes, known as the Christmas Bombing, after which the North seems to have concluded that the details would not matter in the end.

A final agreement was signed in Paris on 27 January 1973, embodying terms that both sides had rejected many times in the past, and might as easily have accepted. The United States agreed to the continued presence of organized communist forces in the South, while the North recognized Thieu's regime, and gave up its demand for a coalition government. Once American forces had gone, the reunification of Vietnam was to be carried out 'step by step through peaceful means, without coercion'. Thieu regarded the treaty as tantamount to surrender. Nixon promised that he would respond with 'full force' if the North failed to comply. He also reminded Thieu of what had happened to Diem.

Saigon fell in April 1975, in an operation indistinguishable from the Easter Offensive, except for its result. Nixon had by then been swept from office in the Watergate affair, a débâcle ultimately attributable to official criminality inspired by the anti-war movement. No American planes appeared, having been grounded by a Congress unwilling to hear any more about the demands of honour, a term sullied in a bad cause. Although there will always be some who imagine that the South might have survived indefinitely, but for American disillusionment, such an argument begs the question of how the Southern regime came to exist in the first place, and why it should have found it so difficult to defend itself.

It is a striking and often overlooked fact that, given twenty years and the backing of the strongest country on earth, the South never came close to producing an army capable of holding the North at bay for even a few months. This is a matter of more than military significance, and goes to the basic legitimacy of a government created, and sustained throughout its existence, by the United States. In the final analysis, it is difficult to avoid concluding that the question of who spoke for the people of Vietnam had been settled, for practical purposes, by the ascendancy of the Viet Minh in 1945, and that the wars fought there over the next thirty years were brought about by the refusal first of the French, and then of the Americans, to accept this perhaps misguided but undoubtedly authentic verdict.

CONCLUSION

Afghanistan and Post-National Conflict

A Chechen woman and a Russian tank, heading in opposite directions. The claims of nationality acknowledge no statute of limitations. The Chechens were conquered by the Russians around the time of the Crimean War, and have resented it ever since.

Afghanistan and Post-National Conflict

> He knew what those jubilant crowds did not know but could
> have learned from books: that the plague bacillus never dies or
> disappears for good; that it can lie dormant for years and years
> in furniture and linen-chests; that it bides its time in bedrooms,
> cellars, trunks and bookshelves; and that perhaps the day would
> come when, for the bane and enlightening of men, it roused up
> its rats again and sent them out to die in a happy city.
>
> – *Albert Camus,* The Plague

IF POLITICS IS about choices, then it almost goes without saying that, absent liberty, morally serious politics is impossible. Yet liberty is the solution to but one problem, and that is bondage. Its achievement does not assure other forms of success, and may unleash waves of violence that traditional or externally imposed authority had held in check. Goethe, whose long life coincided with the first age of revolutions in the eighteenth and nineteenth centuries, concluded that all forms of freedom that do not contribute to self-mastery are pernicious, an observation about the lives of individuals that applies with equal force to those of societies.

The idea that nations require and deserve freedom is a Western idea, as is the specific political construction, the 'nation-state', by which the freedom of nations is supposed to be realized. In contemplating the widespread instability that has followed the spread of nationalism around the globe, its origins are worth remembering; not to suggest that it is a parochial idea – the ubiquity of its appeal shows that it is not – but simply that its historical emergence was dependent upon conditions that are not universal. In political terms, the distinctive feature of Western Civilization in its formative centuries was neither ethnic homogeneity nor an exaggerated regard for the rights of individuals, but rather the existence – in lieu of universal empire, such as prevailed in every other comparably developed region on earth – of strong, mutually competitive, centralized states, to which the centrifugal forces of society were progressively and often forcibly subordinated. The proposition that states could best legitimize themselves by basing their power on an underlying cultural community – the nation – arose long after the power of the state as such had become a settled fact of European history.

This raised awkward problems for those who asserted the primacy of nationality in politics – who held, in other words, that it is nations that create states, and that once cultural communities were freed from external bondage, their natural capacity to organize power would become apparent. Any realistic reading of the historical record, as accumulated in the West, reveals a far more complex process, by which political authority and national identity constitute each other though intense interaction. Nevertheless, the triumph of the national idea in the West cast a shadow over the persistence of colonial tutelage elsewhere, intensely so during the period when the collapse of Europe into war and genocide was rendering its global ascendancy impracticable. National self-determination became a by-word of international politics in the twentieth century less because it promised a clear path to the future than because all other possibilities had been overtaken by events.

The wars of national liberation surveyed in this volume were fought to throw off the vestiges of European empires, or to fill the vacuums of power that decolonization and global cataclysm created. Many of the conflicts that resulted became more violent and consequential than they otherwise might have because Western powers sought to ensure that the chief beneficiaries were not communists or others whose outlook was inimical to Western values. The fact that demands for national liberation were initially advanced, in nearly all cases, by highly mobilized minorities gave Western scepticism a democratic aspect, more plausibly so in some cases than others. To this must be added widespread anxiety about the viability of governments born in such

The ghostly, elegiac, and in this view slightly ominous Korean War Memorial in Washington, DC. Like most Western commemorations of war in recent times, it honours those who fought, with little or no reference to their cause.

forced and contested circumstances, a concern that, however strongly coloured by prejudice and material interest, can scarcely be dismissed in retrospect.

Within this framework both communism and liberalism were stigmatized as 'imperialist' by their opponents, and it was against this somewhat chimerical background that Third World nationalism acquired its distinctive colouration, as a way forward amidst the rocks and shoals of ideology. As those rocks and shoals have receded into the past, however, the romance of national liberation has given way to the hard-scrabble work of state-building, economic development, and the peaceful conciliation of social diversity and political dissent, tasks at which post-colonial regimes have often fallen short, sometimes catastrophically so.

The attitude of advanced societies toward the failed states of the Third World has been inconsistent, to say the least. Although developed countries have shown themselves ready to provide humanitarian aid to new nations in distress, such assistance by definition does not address underlying causes, and depends for its delivery upon the prior restoration of minimally peaceful conditions. The disillusionments of empire and the brutalities of decolonization have combined to place formidable obstacles in the way of those who would use lethal force to impose order on others. From the vantage point of the West, conflicts arising among its former clients and dependencies now appear intractably exotic, rooted in ancient animosities and obscure quarrels into which outsiders intrude at their peril, and for which the blunt instruments of war offer no solution. These apprehensions are reinforced by international law, which affords scant means of legitimizing armed intervention in the internal affairs of even the most reprehensible state.

To which must be added a distinct weariness at the sheer number of crises to be addressed. Even if one sets an almost inhumanly high standard for action – not merely criminal corruption and malfeasance, but mass slaughter and genocide – a consistent policy of 'peace enforcement' in the liberated hinterlands of Europe's old imperia would, in recent years, have required the indefinite garrisoning of Abkhazia, Angola, Bosnia, Burundi, Congo, Haiti, Kashmir, Kosovo, Liberia, Nagorno-Karabakh, Rwanda, Sierra Leone, and Somalia. Even the United States, the only country capable of projecting military power everywhere on this (incomplete) list, lacks the wherewithal to do so. Given the need to make choices and assign priorities, the Americans and their allies have fallen back on traditional calculations of national interest – security, economic growth, Great-Power comity, and so forth – a calculus that has yielded uncertain results for the simple reason that, however calamitous a small state's failure may be for its inhabitants, the consequences for the larger world have always seemed small.

This judgment has been revised by unfolding events in Afghanistan, though the true scope and nature of the revision will remain unclear for some time. Afghanistan's story is different from the other cases discussed in this book, but not so categorically that it will not sound familiar.

Afghanistan is not a new state created by decolonization. Its existence dates from 1747, when the Pashtun tribes living in the shadow of the Hindu Kush set up one of their own as king. The Afghan lands, athwart the ancient Silk Road linking Europe and Asia, were compounded from the corners of three decrepit empires – the Persian Savafids, the Indian Moguls, and the Uzbek Janids – and have always been home to a wide variety of ethnic and linguistic groups, of which the Pashtuns are the largest. Proverbially, Afghanistan is supposed to have been assembled by God out of bits and pieces left over from the rest of creation. The ramshackle quality of His handiwork would be amplified by forbidding terrain, which proved a barrier to foreign penetration, and a reinforcement to the clannishness of the country's inhabitants, whose mutual suspicions would be heightened by physical isolation. A unifying element was provided by the near-universal adherence of the population to Islam, of a populist and juridically tolerant sort in which the key role was played by the village mullahs, or teachers. These became an important prop to a weakly centralized monarchical regime.

In the nineteenth century Afghanistan became a bone of contention between Russia and Great Britain. Their struggle for mastery in Central Asia, know to history as 'the Great Game', gradually brought Afghanistan into the British orbit, though never, strictly speaking, into its empire. The Great Game left its mark on the country by virtue of the methods by which it was played: a combination of bribery, cooptation, and punitive warfare, calculated to exacerbate the Afghans' already debilitating tendency toward internecine strife, and obstruct the consolidation of power in Kabul.

British influence was thrown off when its grip was loosened by the First World War. Afterwards Afghanistan hewed to a policy of strict neutrality and slow modernization. The pace quickened in 1973, when a sharp decline in the country's economic fortunes brought about a coup in which the last Pashtun king was overthrown by a group of leftist civil servants and military officers. Within a few years these had fallen out murderously among themselves, in part over whether Afghanistan should adhere more closely to the Soviet Union, or reach out to the other Muslim states of the region. It was to settle this question that the Soviets invaded at the end of 1979.

The Soviet–Afghan War lasted ten years, and is remembered, fairly enough, as a contest of David and Goliath, in which the designs of a well-armed and powerful army were thwarted by the courageous tenacity of the people in arms. The Soviets certainly did not think they were stepping off a cliff when they moved against their small southern neighbour. Similar interventions against East Germany (1953), Hungary (1958), and Czechoslovakia (1968) had gone smoothly enough. In Afghanistan, too, the Soviets quickly gained control of the major cities, and encountered no difficulty in establishing a puppet regime under men of their choosing. This accomplished, they intended to work their way outward into the provincial capitals, while rebuilding the Afghan national army, to which the final restoration of Kabul's now-compliant authority would be turned over in due course.

The pacification of the Afghan countryside brought ruin to the Soviet war effort, if not, indeed, to the Soviet state, whose collapse a few years after the last of its troops had been withdrawn is widely held to have been hastened by the appalling performance of its most illustrious institution, the Red Army. In all about 640,000 Soviet soldiers served in Afghanistan. Of these 15,000 died or disappeared, a by-no-means excessive toll by then-prevailing standards, but not the decisive one in measuring Soviet performance. For that, one must consider the additional 470,000 casualties suffered from wounds, accidents, or debilitating disease, an almost inconceivable toll for the armed forces of a modern society – which is, of course, precisely what the Soviet Union had failed to become.

Comparisons between the Soviet war in Afghanistan and America's misbegotten intervention in Vietnam soon became commonplace, though the comparison should not be overdrawn. Soviet tactics, like those of the Americans in Southeast Asia, relied excessively on indiscriminate firepower by heavy weapons. Soviet troops rarely entered any area that had not been pulverized in advance – many never left the comparative safety of their tanks – and so found themselves repeatedly thwarted by illusive guerillas who did not hesitate to

Mujahidin graves outside an Afghan refugee camp in Pakistan, 1987.

abandon any position their opponents might choose to attack. That said, however, it must be added that the Soviet problem was, in tactical terms, far simpler than that of the United States. There was no force in Afghanistan comparable to the regular divisions of the People's Liberation Army, hence no large-scale combat by which the work of counter-insurgency could be derailed. Like their American counterparts, however, the Soviets suffered badly from their inability to isolate their adversaries from international assistance. The last straw seems to have been the decision by the United States, taken in 1986, to equip the Afghan resistance with shoulder-fired surface-to-air missiles, an inconsiderable thing in itself, but demoralizing because it mooted what had been the most successful element of the Soviet campaign: the use of helicopters and low-flying aircraft to cut off small bands of guerillas lurking in otherwise impassable terrain.

Three years later the last Soviet troops were gone, and the Afghans were left to themselves. By then, however, the tenuous bonds of Afghan nationhood had been stretched to the breaking point. Afghan resistance to the Soviet invasion had never coalesced into anything like a national liberation front. On the contrary, it had fractionated into jihad, Holy War, and was propelled forward by a combination of religious zeal and tribal loyalty, which lost none of their force when the Soviets left. Thus the victorious mujahidin fell upon each other, a spectacle from which the rest of the world turned away in ill-considered disgust. What was left of the economy collapsed, and social violence became endemic. Millions fled, most to Pakistan and Iran, and by the early 1990s Afghanistan's future as an organized polity was decidedly in doubt.

It was among the masses of refugees created by the Afghan civil war that the ultimate victors in that conflict would emerge. These were the Taliban ('seekers'), formed in September, 1994 by students and graduates from the Islamic schools (madrassas) that had grown up along the Afghan-Pakistan border. Most Taliban were Pashtun, a fact that would hamper their ability to control Afghanistan's northern-most provinces, where other groups predominated. Their programme, however, purported to transcend ethnic differences, by uniting the country's warring tribes under the banner of Islamic law, to whose remorseless application they committed themselves without reserve.

A surprising number of Western observers attributed the Taliban's ascendancy – they would eventually control about three-quarters of Afghanistan – to the power of ideas. Superficially, their programme exuded a kind of Cromwellian strictness that probably appealed more to world-weary outsiders than it did to the Afghans themselves, who knew that much of what was being propounded as Qur'anic law was simply the ignorant misanthropy of the Pashtun village. In reality, the Taliban prevailed over their rivals chiefly because of the support they received from Pakistan, a country with a large Pashtun population of its own, and one with a strong interest in having a weak and obliging neighbour to its north; also, less conspicuously, from Saudi Arabia, whose conservative élites have long protected themselves from the predations of radical Islamism by exporting it to the remoter corners of the Muslim world.

This latter connection would, indirectly, prove fatal to the Taliban regime, owing to its decision to lend its protection to the al-Qaida terrorist organization. Al-Qaida ('the Base') is the creation of renegade Saudi businessman Osama bin Laden. Bin Laden first went to Afghanistan to fight the Soviets in 1979, and later helped organize a global network to funnel arms and recruits into the country. Al-Qaida was founded in 1988 as a successor to this organization, with a view to supporting Islamist movements in the Persian Gulf, and to projecting the work of jihad on to a larger stage. Its activities would soon make Bin Laden the most famous outlaw on earth.

Bin Laden returned to Afghanistan in the spring of 1996, having been expelled most recently from Sudan, where his presence had become intolerable after the UN threatened to impose sanctions in connection with an attempt on the life of Egyptian President Hosni Mubarak. The Taliban, despite their enthusiasm for bin Laden's cause, were by no means blind to the danger his arrival posed, and affected to have taken him in so as to keep him under wraps. In reality, however, the organizational and financial means at bin Laden's disposal far exceeded those of his beleaguered hosts, who grew increasingly dependent upon him. In 1999 the Taliban threw away what would prove to be their last chance for international legitimacy when they refused a Security Council demand to turn bin Laden over to competent outside authorities.

This demand was repeated in September of 2001, following al-Qaida's attack on the Pentagon and New York's World Trade Center, in which over 3,000 people were killed. A second refusal followed, compounded of Islamic zealotry, a misguided belief in the solidarity of the Muslim world, and the commonplace mythologies of a people that, having known little but war in its history, had come to imagine that it was invincible. The result was swift annihilation at the hands of the United States, in a campaign of lapidary precision and ferocity that destroyed the Taliban and left al-Qaida's network degraded and dispersed – though in the immediate aftermath the leaders of both remained unaccounted for, and presumably at large. Afghanistan passed into UN receivership under an interim government, backed by peacekeepers provided chiefly by America's European allies. How, or even whether, it will emerge is anyone's guess.

It is much too soon to draw any but the most tentative conclusions from this sorry tale, not least because it is far from over. That it illustrates the perils of indifference to the fate of small nations seems obvious; likewise the perils that may befall small nations whose territories become bastions for international criminal conspiracy. Yet the true scale and nature of the threat are murky, and likely to remain so for some time. The immediate inference of the United States, that it was now at war with 'terrorism', will almost certainly prove inadequate. Terrorism is at once too fungible and too narrowly tactical a concept to serve as the basis for a long-term strategy, in the same way that 'jungle warfare' proved to be a poor vehicle for understanding revolutionary insurgency. The West's last great strategic vision – the containment of communism – took at least a decade to emerge even in rough outline, in part because its development depended upon radically new military means – nuclear weapons – whose application was hard to understand. Although it would be wrong to assume that the challenge posed by radical Islamism will rise to the level of global communism, it is a safe bet that the gravity of the threat and the complexity of the strategic response it requires will be in rough proportion to each other.

Not the least startling aspect of Afghanistan's dissolution was the role of American military power in its final stage. The wars of national liberation were a disillusionment for Western arms, to the point where it had become commonplace to portray the military capacities of advanced societies as practically irrelevant. This point of view was strengthened when the Cold War ended not with a bang, but in a vast going-out-of-business sale, clear evidence, as it seemed, that the arbitrament of world affairs had passed from the battlefield to the marketplace. Recent events in Afghanistan, Kosovo, Bosnia, and elsewhere have cast doubt on this conclusion, while suggesting that the true gap between the best modern armed forces, specifically those of the United State, and those of the developing world, is now closer to what prevailed in the Age of Empire than in more recent times.

This alone makes it safe to assume that war will retain its place in international life for some time to come. War's object, moreover, is likely to remain a familiar one: the protection of nations against the predation of outsiders and the rapacity of their leaders. Afghanistan, it must be emphasized, was ruined not by the passions of nationality – whose dangers have been fully displayed elsewhere in this volume – but by their absence, certainly by their weakness in relation to the claims of tribalism on the one hand, and a supra-national religious fanaticism on the other. Not the least of the many paradoxes arising from the wars of national liberation is that, for all the misery and folly that attended them, the creation of states governed by, and genuinely answerable to, their inhabitants, remains mankind's best hope for a decent future, and one for which people seem certain to keep fighting.

Biographical notes

Ben Bella, Ahmed (1916–)

The central figure among those who planned the outbreak of the Algerian Revolution in 1954. He was imprisoned in 1950 for robbing a bank to finance nationalist agitation, but escaped two years later and fled to Egypt. There he became the main organizer of foreign assistance to the FLN. He was captured in 1956, and remained in prison until shortly before the end of the war, a circumstance that freed him from blame for the failings of FLN military leadership. He became President of Algeria in 1963 thanks to the backing of the army, which overthrew him two years later.

Ben-Gurion, David (1886–1973)

The dominant figure among the founders of the state of Israel, becoming that country's first Prime Minister in 1948, having previously served thirteen years as head of the Jewish Agency in Palestine. He was born David Gruen in Russian Poland, and emigrated to Palestine in 1906. He was expelled for Zionist activity by the Ottoman government in 1914, but returned three years later as a member of the British Army's Jewish Legion. His confidence in British sympathy collapsed when the British restricted Jewish immigration and land ownership in the 1930s, though he favoured continued co-operation as long as the Nazi threat in Europe existed. His cultivation of international Jewish support, above all in the United States, and his success in suppressing Irgun and other radical groups, were essential contributions to Israeli success in 1948. As Prime Minister he took a hard line against Arab terrorism, and met ceasefire violations with stiff reprisals, a policy culminating in the pre-emptive attack against Egypt in 1956.

CASTRO, FIDEL (1927–)

Born the son of a sugar planter, he trained as a lawyer, and found his way to political action by way of representing indigent suspects in Havana. In 1953 he led an attack on an army barracks, for which he was briefly imprisoned. Released as part of a general amnesty, he moved to Mexico, from where he returned at the head of a small revolutionary band in 1956. At the time of his triumph three years later, his reputation was closer to Garibaldi's than to Lenin's. His increasingly open embrace of communism thereafter brought him the implacable enmity of the United States, and involved his country in one of the most dangerous crises of the Cold War in 1962, when he acceded to the provision of nuclear-armed Soviet missile bases in Cuba. His promotion of revolution elsewhere in Latin America, and his willingness to lend Cuban troops as Soviet proxies in Angola, contributed to his personal standing as a major Third World leader, without appreciably advancing the interests of Cuba itself.

CHIANG KAI-SHEK (1887–1975)

Succeeded Sun Yat-sen as leader of the Kuomintang in 1925. His suppression of the warlords created the basis for a revived Chinese national state, established in Nanjing in 1928 with Chiang as President. His hold on power was never complete, however, owing to endemic factionalism within the KMT, rivalry with the Communists and conflict with Japan. In 1936 he was kidnapped by dissident officers, and forced to accept a united front with the Communists against the Japanese, who invaded the following year. He was the recognized leader of China throughout the Second World War. Afterwards, however, the United States proved unwilling to intervene to save his regime from the Communists. Although he never gave up hope of an American-sponsored return to the mainland, Chiang passed the last twenty-five years of his life as President of the rump national government on Taiwan, where he oversaw the beginning of that island's remarkably rapid economic modernization.

GANDHI, MOHANDAS (1869–1948)

The father of the Indian nation state, he first became involved in political activism in South Africa in 1907, where he organized resistance to official discrimination against Indian settlers. He returned to India in 1915, and became a leader of the Congress movement. He is associated above all with methods of non-violent protest, including boycotts, marches, civil disobedience, hunger strikes and other gestures calculated to delegitimize India's British rulers, and sow self-doubt among them. Repeated periods of imprisonment only strengthened his moral authority, as did his personal asceticism. His followers dubbed him Mahatma ('Great Soul'), though some were disillusioned by his eventual acceptance of partition as the only way to avoid inter-communal violence (which came anyway). He was assassinated by a Hindu fanatic.

GUEVARA, ERNESTO 'CHE' (1928–67)

The son of a prosperous Argentine family, he trained as a doctor, and practised briefly before being radicalized by the American intervention in Guatemala in 1954. He joined Castro during the latter's exile in Mexico, and held a variety of improbable positions (President of the Cuban National Bank, Minister of Industries) following Castro's victory in 1959. In 1965 Guevara left Cuba for the jungles of Bolivia, hoping to foment revolution among the tin miners there. He made little headway, and was eventually captured and killed by Bolivian troops. Guevara's writings on guerrilla war became world famous, while his face, captured in an oft-reproduced photograph by Alberto Diaz Gutierrez, has become synonymous with the romance of revolution.

HO CHI MINH (1890–1969)

Born Nguyen Sinh Cung, the son of a provincial official, the name under which he became famous ('Ho, the Seeker of Light') was one of several revolutionary pseudonyms he adopted over the years. He travelled widely as a young man, when he worked, among other things, as a merchant seaman. He arrived in Paris in 1917, and became a leading figure on the French Left. He petitioned the Versailles peacemakers demanding self-determination for Vietnam, and later helped found the French Communist Party. He studied in Moscow in the 1920s, and thereafter worked as a revolutionary organizer in the Soviet Union, China, and Indo-China, where he helped found the Vietnamese (later Indo-Chinese) Communist Party (1930) and the anti-Japanese resistance movement known as the Viet Minh (1941). From 1945 to his death in 1969, Ho was the pre-eminent figure in the Vietnamese communist movement, to which he contributed an exceptional capacity to balance military and political requirements, and great skill in managing North Vietnam's critical relationships with the Soviet Union and China.

KIM IL-SUNG (1912–94)

Leader of the North Korean state from its founding in 1948 until his death in 1994. He rose to prominence as a member of the Korean anti-Japanese guerrilla movement in Manchuria, where he attracted the attention of Soviet military advisers in the 1930s. He led a Korean contingent of the Soviet Red Army during the Second World War, in which guise he returned to Korea as part of the Soviet occupation force in 1945. His efforts to unify Korea by force failed, but left him securely in power in the North, where he became the object of an intense personality cult. Even by communist standards, Kim's regime was distinguished by autocracy, economic autarchy and the most extreme cultural isolation.

MAO TSE-TUNG (1893–1976)

Mao was born in Hunan, the son of prosperous peasants. He discovered Marxism while working as a librarian in Beijing, and helped found the

Chinese Communist Party in 1921. He was among the first Communist leaders to collaborate with the Kuomintang, and to urge a revolutionary strategy based upon the peasantry rather than the proletariat. His ascendancy within the Chinese communist movement dates from the Long March in 1934–5, though his authority was not absolute until the 1960s, when the Cultural Revolution (1965–8) established the cult of personality with which his later career is synonymous. Overrated as a theorist, Mao's true gifts were for practical leadership, which he exercised with great cunning and ruthlessness.

Nasser, Gamal Abdel (1918–70)

A leading figure in the military coup that overthrew Egypt's King Farouk in 1952, he became prime minister in 1954, and president two years later. He sought to promote economic modernization in Egypt, and non-alignment and 'pan-Arabism' abroad. His ambitions inspired suspicion among other Arab leaders and brought him into conflict with Britain, from whom he wrested control of the Suez Canal, and the United States, which he sought to play off against the Soviet Union. He was also an active promoter of socialist and nationalist movements in Africa. His losing wars with Israel (1956 and 1967) diminished his reputation, though at the time of his death in 1970 he was still reckoned among the most formidable of Third World leaders.

Ngo Dinh Diem (1901–63)

President of South Vietnam from 1955 until his assassination in 1963. He came from an old aristocratic family, which converted to Catholicism in the seventeenth century. He served briefly as Interior Minister under the last emperor, Bao Dai, in 1933, but left because he found it impossible to work with the French. In 1945 Ho Chi Minh invited him to join the

Viet Minh government in Hanoi, in order to appeal to Catholic opinion. Diem refused, and lived abroad during the decade of war that followed. As head of the US-backed government in the South, he refused to hold the national elections called for by the Geneva Accords that ended the first Indo-China War. Instead, he set up an autocratic regime in the South, which did little to redress the social grievances from which the communist movement drew its energy. At the same time, his heavy reliance on Catholics to run the country offended and alarmed the Buddhist majority. Although his regime fared poorly against an escalating communist threat, it was his brutal treatment of the Buddhists, whom he imagined to be in league with the North, that cost him the confidence of the United States, which tacitly approved the *coup d'état* in which he was killed.

Vo Nguyen Giap (1912–)

Giap was the senior commander of Vietnamese communist forces in both Indo-China Wars. He was a revolutionary nationalist from his early teens, an attitude that was strengthened by the death of his first wife and her sister at the hands of the French. Giap taught history for a time at the Lycée in Hanoi, and professed great admiration for Napoleon. The more profound influence was certainly Mao, whose ideas about protracted war underlay Giap's strategy. The maddening combination of revolutionary insurgency and conventional operations that defeated both the French and the United States was largely his conception. As a commander, Giap's outstanding characteristics were his willingness to employ terror and torture to control and radicalize the civilian population, and his iron determination to succeed in the face of terrible losses.

Further reading

A good account of Chinese history from the fall of the Manchus to the rise of Mao is John K. Fairbank and Albert Feuerwerker, eds., *The Cambridge History of China*, volume 13, part 2: *Republican China, 1912–1949* (1986). Military dimensions are treated in Edward L. Dreyer, *China at War, 1901–1949* (1995). An important recent work on the warlord period and its consequences is Arthur Waldron, *From War to Nationalism: China's Turning Point, 1924–1925* (1995). The best history of the communist ascendancy is Tony Saich, *The Rise to Power of the Chinese Communist Party* (1996). On the war that brought them to power, see Suzanne Pepper, *Civil War in China: The Political Struggle, 1945–1949* (1978; reprinted 1999), and Stephen Levine, *Anvil of Victory: The Communist Revolution in Manchuria, 1945–1948* (1987).

Among many general histories of the Korean War, Max Hastings, *The Korean War* (1987), stands out for graceful writing, and William Stueck, *The Korean War: An International History* (1995), for analytic breadth. D. Clayton James, *Refighting the Last War: Command and Crisis in Korea, 1950–1953* (1993), deals with American decision-making. China's intervention has been well-studied by Chen Jian, *China's Road to the Korean War* (1994), and Shu Guang Zhang, *Mao's Military Romanticism: China and the Korean War, 1950–1953* (1995). The origins of the war are surveyed in Peter Lowe, *The Origins of the Korean War* (1986), and in greater depth, from a (mainly North) Korean perspective, by Bruce Cumings, *The Origins of the Korean War*, 2 volumes (1981–90).

A comprehensive study of the French war in Indo-China is Jacques Dalloz, *The War in Indo-China, 1945–54*, translated by Josephine Bacon (1990), which can be read along with Bernard Fall's more circumstantial accounts, *Street Without Joy* (1964) and *Hell in a Very Small Place* (1966). The latter is still the best account of Dien Bien Phu. William J. Duiker's *The Communist Road to Power in Vietnam* (1981) is indispensable on Northern strategy. It treats the American phase of the war as well. Duiker's earlier work on *Vietnamese Anti-Colonialism* (1971) remains important as an exploration of the Viet Minh's ascendancy. Likewise the more recent books by Greg Lockhart, *Nation in Arms: The Origins of the People's Army of Vietnam*

(1989), and David Marr, *Vietnam, 1945: The Quest for Power* (1995). No other conflict in Southeast Asia has been studied as well as Indo-China; but there is a good recent study of Malaya by Donald Mackay, *The Malayan Emergency, 1948–1960* (1997). For Indonesia, see Anthony Reid, *The Indonesian National Revolution, 1945–1950* (1974; reprinted 1986).

There is a concise account of the Algerian war in Anthony Clayton, *The Wars of French Decolonization* (1994), which also has good chapters on Indo-China. The pre-eminent study is Alistair Horne, *A Savage War of Peace: Algeria, 1954–1962* (1977), which may be supplemented by Michael Kettle, *De Gaulle and Algeria, 1940–1960* (1993). Alf Andrew Heggoy, *Insurgency and Counter-Insurgency in Algeria* (1972), is excellent on tactical and operational issues. Peter Paret's incisive *French Revolutionary Warfare from Indochina to Algeria* (1964) has lost nothing with the passage of time.On post-colonial conflict in Africa, see John Darwin, *The End of the British Empire* (1991), John Hargreaves, *Decolonization in Africa* (1988), Henry Wilson, *African Decolonization* (1994), and Anthony Clayton, *Frontiersmen: Warfare in Africa Since 1950* (1999). John de St Jorre, *The Nigerian Civil War* (1972) is comprehensive on military, social and political issues. John Stremlau, *The International Politics of the Nigerian Civil War, 1967–1970* (1977), deals with the reactions of outsiders. For Angola and Mozambique there are David Birmingham, *Portugal and Africa* (1999), James Ciment, *Angola and Mozambique: Postcolonial Wars in Southern Africa* (1997), and the relevant chapters in Malyn Newitt's *A History of Mozambique* (1995). The best account of the 1971 India–Pakistan war is Richard Sisson and Leo E. Rose, *War and Secession: Pakistan, India, and the Creation of Bangladesh* (1990).

Among histories of the Cuban Revolution one should compare the critical account by William E. Ratliff, *Castroism and Communism in Latin America, 1959–1976* (1976), and the more sympathetic treatment by Marifeli Perez-Stable, *The Cuban Revolution: Origins, Course, and Legacy* (1998). Che Guevara has come in for a compendious if somewhat uncritical biography by Jon Anderson Lee, *Che Guevara: A Revolutionary Life* (1997). On the wars of Central America, see James Dunkerley, *The Long War: Dictatorship and Revolution in El Salvador* (revd edn, 1985), and Thomas Walker, ed., *Revolution & Counterrevolution in Nicaragua* (1991).

Chaim Herzog, *The Arab–Israeli Wars* (1982), is detailed and surprisingly dry. On the Israeli Defence Force, see Martin Van Creveld, *The Sword and the Olive: A Critical History of the Israeli Defense Force* (1998), which does not entirely supercede the earlier work by Edward Luttwak and Dan Horowitz, *The Israeli Army* (1975). William Roger Louis, *The British Empire in the Middle East, 1945–1951: Arab Nationalism, the United States, and Postwar Imperialism* (1984), is essential on the British role. The early history of Israel's nuclear programme is well studied in Avner Cohen, *Israel and the Bomb* (1998). On American involvement, see David Schoenbaum, *The United States and the State of Israel* (1993). Anita Shapira's splendid *Land and Power: The Zionist Resort to Force, 1881–1948* (1992), casts a useful light on subsequent events.

George C. Herring, *America's Longest War: The United States and Vietnam, 1950–1975* (3rd edn, revd 1996), remains the best introduction to the American war in Vietnam. Eric M. Bergerud, *The Dynamics of Defeat: The Vietnam War in Hau Nghia Province* (1991), provides a good view from the ground, and Mark Clodfelter, *The Limits of Air Power: The American Bombing of North Vietnam* (1989), from the air. Two important new studies of America's self-entanglement are Fredrik Logevall, *Choosing War: The Lost Chance for Peace and the Escalation of the Vietnam War* (1999), and David Kaiser's ground-breaking *American Tragedy: Kennedy, Johnson, and the Origins of the Vietnam War* (2000). Jonathan Shay, *Achilles in Vietnam* (1994), offers some strikingly original reflections on the warrior's moral universe.

The best accounts of the Afghan civil war are Larry P. Goodson, Afghanistan's *Endless War* (2001), and Ahmed Rashid, *Taliban* (2000), both written before the al-Qaida attacks of September 2001. Robert Kaplan's *Soldiers of God* (2001), which recounts his experiences among the mujahidin in the 1980s, has lost not of its incisiveness. Among a mass of hastily written journalistic accounts of al-Qaida, see Peter Bergen, *Holy War, Inc.* (2001).

Index

Picture credits

Every effort has been made to contact the copyright holders for images reproduced in this book. The publishers would welcome any errors or omissions being brought to their attention.

Corbis: pp. 2, 66; 6, 180, 196–7 Tim Page. Bettmann: pp. 21, 24, 41, 51, 55, 78, 81, 105, 111, 124, 155, 173, 175, 193, 204–5, 218–19, 241; 22, 33, 62–3, 72–3, 77, 89, 140, 146, 170–71 Hulton-Deutsch Collection; 36–7 Ward; 39, 45 Underwood & Underwood; 108–109, 121 Marc Garanger; 137 Leonard de Selva; 162 Tom Bean; 167 Bill Gentile; 185, 190–91 David Rubinger; 194 Jeffrey L Rotman; 228 Todd Gipstein; 232–3 Zen Icknow. AKG: pp. 18–19, 118–9, 206, 220. Camera Press: pp. 27, 58, 84–5, 93, 98, 116, 128–9, 131, 151, 152–3, 165, 168, 186, 187, 199, 200, 203, 210–211, 212–13, 217, 221, 222, 224–5, 242.

The drawings on page 216 are by Peter Smith and Malcolm Swanston of Arcadia Editions.